Theme Paper
on
'One Nation, One Election'

Sixty Eighth Members' Annual Conference 2024

Dr Sapna Chadah
Associate Professor of Constitutional
and Administrative Law
IIPA, New Delhi

Indian Institute of Public Administration

Prints Publications Pvt Ltd

Published by

Prints Publications Pvt Ltd
Viraj Tower-2, 4259/3, Ansari Road,
Darya Ganj, New Delhi-110002, India.
Phone : 91-11-45355555
E-mail: contact@printspublications.com

Edition: 2025

ISBN: 978-93-6697-840-6

Published and Printed by Mr. Pranav Gupta (Managing Director) on behalf of Prints Publications Pvt Ltd, New Delhi.

भारतीय लोक प्रशासन संस्थान
Indian Institute of Public Administration
Indraprastha Estate, Ring Road, New Delhi-110002
www.iipa.org.in

Surendra Nath Tripathi, IAS (Retd.)
Director General
(Former Secretary, M/o Parliamentary Affairs, GoI)

Foreword

In a representative democracy elections are a sacred political exercise. They are a very vital part of the political process which emanates from the fundamental assumption that people are sovereign. Elections provide an opportunity to take stock of work done by the government and for reposing their confidence in a political party or for its withdrawal. It is, therefore, an essential condition for the success of democracy that people maintain their allegiance towards the democratic institutions based on rule of law. Obviously, 'Free and fair elections' are the indicator of such allegiance. A satisfactory election mechanism should ensure that the selected leaders are actually representative, responsible and responsive.

Election system being one of the major instruments of translating political democracy into action, as well as an instrument that reflects economic and social democratic system prevailing in the country needs to be adequately reformed and made flawless. Electoral reforms are necessary for the success and survival of parliamentary democracy in our country. Electoral reform is a continuous process. However, lately the reform of electoral process in India has been engaging the attention of many thinkers, academicians, political parties, Members of Parliament and Legislatures and laymen. In what way should our electoral system be reformed so as to ensure a fair and just election and a better representation of the popular will?

In a significant move towards electoral reform, the Union Cabinet under NDA has approved the proposal to conduct simultaneous elections for the Lok Sabha, State Assemblies, and local government bodies. Certainty in governance is crucial for effective decision-making and sustained development. Synchronised elections can help avoid policy paralysis and create a favorable environment for progress. However, there are doubts being raised by some about its implementation in terms of logistics, Constitutional amendments, federalism concerns, eroding regional diversity, etc.

To provide a platform to discuss the nuances of simultaneous elections and its implementation in India, the 68th Members' Annual Conference of IIPA for the year 2024 is being organized on the theme "One Nation One Election". The theme paper brings out the need, importance, and challenges in implementing synchronized elections in India. I appreciate the sincere efforts of Dr. Sapna Chadah, Associate Professor of Constitutional & Administrative Law, IIPA for writing an insightful theme paper. We are highly obliged to Dr. Jitendra Singh, Chairman, IIPA, whose guidance and suggestions sustain the momentum for all creative and innovative activities at IIPA.

Place: New Delhi
Date: October 7, 2024

(S. N. Tripathi)
Director General, IIPA

Coordinates: 91-11-23702434 • Fax: +91-11-23702440 • Email: sntripathi@iipa.education | directoriipa9@gmail.com

Preface

The process of election is the corner-stone of any democratic system; it's a device to determine the authority for governance of the country for a defined period. Free and fair elections are heart and soul of the representative form of government and serve as means of communication between the public and the government. Electoral reforms have been an issue of intense debate in contemporary India, particularly in the last one decade. The time has come for us to look at the electoral reforms for improving the system and ensuring free and just elections and better representation of the popular will. Today the problems of greatest interest in connection with elections are frequent elections, requirement of vast election machinery, huge cost and time invested for elections, suspension of development activities due to MCC, regulation of expenditure, registration of voters and election abuses. To streamline the electoral system and procedure, radical reforms are needed. The frequent elections in one or the other part of the country are imposing huge burden on human resources and adversely impacting the economy and development.

The government has accepted the recommendations of High-Level Committee under Chairmanship of Shri Ram Nath Kovind, Former President to hold synchronized elections in the country. This Theme Paper on 'One Nation, One Election' discusses the subtleties of holding simultaneous elections. The paper also brings forth the constitutional and legal provisions for elections, national and international experiences on concurrent elections, the views expressed by various committees on it; and the benefits and challenges of having simultaneous elections.

In bringing out this theme paper, I wish to place on record my sincere gratitude to Shri S. N. Tripathi, Director General, IIPA for giving me the opportunity to write this paper and present it in the Sixty-Eight Members' Annual Conference 2024 of IIPA. I would like to place on record my sincere thanks to Prof Suresh Misra, Professor in Public Administration for his support and guidance in completion of the paper. I am thankful to Shri Amitabh Ranjan, Registrar, IIPA and Shri H. C. Yadav, Librarian in-charge, IIPA for the necessary administrative and academic support. I am indebted to my friends and colleagues at IIPA for the moral support in completing the task. I am thankful to Ms. Meghna, Publication Officer and Ms. Hemlata,

Publication Division for all the support in bringing out the paper in the present form. Last, but not the least, I acknowledge the support received from Ms. Harsh, Research Officer; Mr. Mohd. Uvais, Research Officer, Mr. Nitin, Office Assistant and Mr. Ashok Choudhary, Office Assistant.

Place: New Delhi **Sapna Chadah**

Date: October 7, 2024

Contents

Foreword ... *iii*

Preface ... *v*

Abstract ... **1**

1. Introduction ... **2**

2. Parliamentary Democratic Process and Elections ... **3**

3. Evolution of Parliamentary Democratic Process in India ... **7**

4. Constitutional Provisions to Elections ... **9**

4.1 Provisions relating to the Election of President ... 9

4.2 Election of Vice-President ... 11

4.3 System of Election to Lok Sabha ... 11

4.4 Elections to Rajya Sabha ... 14

4.5 Elections to State Legislatures ... 14

4.6 Composition of the Legislative Councils ... 15

4.7 Adult Suffrage ... 15

5. Election Commission-Role and Functions ... **16**

5.1 Election Commission ... 16

5.2 State Election Commission ... 18

6. Reservation of seats ... **18**

6.1 Reservation of seats in Lok Sabha ... 18

6.2 Reservation of seats in Vidhan Sabha ... 19

7. Elections for Local Self Government Institutions ... **20**

7.1 Elections to Panchayati Raj Institutions ... 20

7.2 Elections for Municipalities ... 23

8. Laws dealing with Elections ... **25**

9.One Nation, One Election ... **27**

9.1 Simultaneous Elections – Meaning and Scope 27
9.2 Models of Simultaneous General Elections 27
9.3 Concurrent Elections-Country Specific Experience............................ 30
9.4 Simultaneous Election –Indian Scenario.. 33
9.5 The First Four General Elections after Independence-Brief............ 36
9.6 Recommendations of Various Committees on Simultaneous Elections 40
9.7 Views Expressed on Simultaneous Elections....................................... 48
9.8 Need for Simultaneous Elections 50
9.9 Challenges for 'One Nation, One Election'.. 56
10. Conclusion 59
11. References... 60
12. Bibliography...68

Theme Paper
on
'One Nation, One Election'

Abstract

"Democracy' and 'free and fair election' are inseparable. Elections are the centerpiece of democracy; it is difficult to visualize democracy without elections. Ensuring free and fair elections is the first prerequisite for the success of democratic process. Elections are a very vital part of the political process which emanates from the fundamental assumption that people are sovereign. In any democracy, the people do want and have every right to change governments according to their wishes, in a peaceful and orderly manner. The little man, in his multitude, making his vote at the poll does a social audit of his Parliament plus political choice of his proxy. Elections give the executive and legislative branches the representative nature they need to reflect the will of the people. The most powerful aspect of democracy unquestionably is the highest number of individuals participating in elections.

India, a Socialist, Secular, Democratic Republic, is the largest democracy in the World. The modern Indian, which came into existence on 15th of August 1947, is a constitutional democracy with a parliamentary system of government. Democracy is one of the inalienable features of the Constitution of India and forms of its basic structure. The concept of democracy as visualised by the Constitution presupposes the representation of the people in Parliament and state legislatures by the method of election. At the heart of the system lies a commitment to hold regular, free and fair elections.

Federal democracies, which are frequently distinguished by the coexistence of national and subnational governmental levels, face a unique challenge-frequency of elections. In the past decades, India is also grappling with the same issue with hundreds of state assembly elections taking place. These frequent elections come at a high cost in terms of money and administrative work and also causing inconvenience to citizens, political parties and government. This has triggered a debate for adoption of 'One Nation, One Election' – simultaneous elections. On September 18, 2024, the Union Cabinet, chaired by the Prime Minister Shri Narendra Modi, accepted the recommendations of the High-Level Committee on Simultaneous Elections under the chairmanship of former President Shri Ram Nath Kovind.

A Constitution has to be a 'living document' that is capable of adapting to changing needs and requirements of people and society. It has to be dynamic, effective and efficient, responding to the changing situations and growing needs of the citizens and meeting their expectations. However, at the same time the intrinsic values and basic features of the Constitution, such as democracy, free and fair elections and federalism cannot be compromised. In this background we need to examine and to implement the 'one nation, one election' rule; introducing reforms in the domain of the electoral system without damaging the intrinsic character and framework of the Constitution. No doubt it is not an easy task; there will always be people who will view the changes with doubt and oppose them, and want the status quo to be continued throughout.

1. Introduction

Everyone believes that politics and political institutions matter. But exactly how they matter, and how one might choose among them, remains something of a mystery. Different political ideas and acts are accepted and rewarded in different political systems while others are rejected and penalized. Depending on the kind of political institutions- totalitarian, authoritarian or democratic-in place makes a difference in people's lives, as each commands its own set of rules and penalties for the ways people engage in politics. The structure of political institutions may also affect the efficacy and sustainability of the institutions themselves. Therefore, choice of political institutions is critical.

Democracy has swept the world, but there are also far-reaching concerns about democracy itself. What should democratic government look like? What institutions will work best? The concept of democracy may be described as that of a system of government—a set of rules under which government is selected and operates- whereby the governed people enjoy control over the governing authority.[1] This idea of democracy lacks precision as it doesn't specifically state what kind or degree of control, and how much control, the people ought to have over the authorities. What kind of influence the public should have over the government? Furthermore, it gives us no information regarding who is a member of the controlling group or who the controlled authorities are. Even if there are unanswered questions, still most will agree that democracy, or at least democracy as ought to be, is a preferred form of government to alternatives like autocracy, or a one-party system etc. Democracy is better to these alternatives as it guarantees equality among citizens, defends people against government infringement on their rights, and gives expression to the will of the people.

Democracy is one of the inalienable features of the Constitution of India and forms of its basic structure.[2] The concept of democracy as visualised by the Constitution presupposes the representation of the people in Parliament and state legislatures by the method of election.[3] The philosophy of democratic elections as narrated by Sir Winston Churchil in matchless words:[4]

> *"At the bottom of all tributes paid to democracy is the little man, walking into a little booth, with a little pencil, making a little cross on a little bit of paper-no amount of rhetoric or voluminous discussion can possibly diminish the overwhelming importance of the point."*

The Supreme Court in *Mohinder Singh Gill & Anr vs The Chief Election* Commissioner has held that:

> *"Democracy is government by the people. It is a continual participative operation, not a cataclysmic, periodic exercise. The little man, in his multitude, making his vote at the poll does a social audit of his Parliament plus political choice of his proxy. Although the full flower of participative government rarely blossoms, the minimum credential of popular government is appeal to the people after every term for a renewal of confidence. So we have adult franchise and general elections as constitutional compulsions".*[5]

2. Parliamentary Democratic Process and Elections

Since participation of each member of the society in governance is unachievable, liberal democratic form of government which allows a mean for peaceful change through election process brings us closest to that ideal. Thus, elections and voting are, universal phenomena in liberal democracies. Elections to Parliament, legislature, and executive have such immense significance because of their authoritative and powerful role in the establishment and functioning of governments, as well as their influence on the lives of the people entrusted to their care. Elections give the executive and legislative branches the representative nature they need to reflect the will of the people. The most powerful aspect of democracy unquestionably is the highest number of individuals participating in elections. Nevertheless, the democratic government's most vulnerable point remains the election process through which it seeks its mandate.

'Election' is "the act of choosing; choice; the act of selecting one or more from others." Hence appropriately, "the act of choosing a person to fill an office or employment, by any manifestation of preference, as by ballot, uplifted hands or viva voce; as the election of a king, of a president, or a mayor. [6] Black's law dictionary defines 'election' as the act of choosing or selecting one or more from a greater number of persons, things, courses, or rights. The choice of an alternative.[7] The Representation of the People Act, 1951 defines the term 'election' as "an election to fill a seat or seats in either House of Parliament or in the House or either House of the Legislature of a State other than the State of Jammu and Kashmir".[8]

"Democracy' and 'free and fair election' are inseparable. Elections are the centerpiece of democracy; it is difficult to visualize democracy without elections. These are the fundamental occasions for most people to get personally involved in politics and the cornerstone political events of democratic society. An election is a discovery process, a way of finding out who will be temporarily in charge of government.[9] An important "function" of elections is their use as a check on power. The purpose of the elections is to choose who will be in charge of government. Elections are primary, if not exclusive, means by which citizenry maintain control over the state. They are important tool for eliminating people from power than keeping them there. Democracy primarily as a means of limiting government protecting the rights of minorities and majorities from arbitrary state action. It is more important for the electorate to be able to remove a bad leader from power and put in place someone who might do a better job. The electoral transfer of power is a defining feature of democracy.

In modern times, elections have become everyday events. In democracy, the objective of the elections is to allow the voters to make their choices and to express their political preferences between the political parties and the candidates. These choices made by the voters have critical implications and consequences for conduct of government and policies government pursue. Elections give an opportunity to the citizens to evaluate the past performance of the government and give a verdict on the same and establish guidelines for future actions of the government. However, researchers and critic of democracy have raised serious doubt over the knowledge and capabilities of the voters to lay down these guidelines for the government.[10] The basic function of elections is legitimization. The citizens thronging to polls in large number to cast their ballot offers legitimation for the regime.

In democracy besides legitimization, elections perform a number of additional functions. Democratic elections provide voters with choice between different contenders for the office concerned, may it be individual candidates or political parties. In an election for decision making body like legislature, elections also determine the relative strength of the political parties to which the candidates belong. As the candidates elected in democratic elections are also incumbent office-bearers, elections also serve the function of *holding these office bearers accountable* for the way they exercised power since previous elections, thereby recording their approval or disapproval of their actions.[11] Election process gives an opportunity to make a choice between the policies proposed by the candidates/ parties in government and their opponents. If the governments are responsive to the choices manifested in election outcomes by the voters, elections serve as guidance tool that may help to bring the course of public policy closer to what voters want. The sight of candidates submitting to the popular will of voters, provides some sense of empowerment to the citizens. Requiring millions of people to express their preferences in a way to yield an intelligible outcome from which a mandate to govern can be derived requires organization, discipline and sophistication.

Wilson[12] and Bagehot[13] more than a century ago complained about the fragmentation, ineffectiveness, and parochialism under separation of powers, and argued that a parliamentary system wherein legislative and executive authority lies in a single leadership group, promotes effective and responsible government. Choices concerning the form of institutions have an impact on nearly all aspects of democratic government. Whether a country chooses a presidential or parliamentary form, it is selecting an entire system, all of whose characteristics emerge automatically from the political dynamics that the selected form initiates, whether the country likes it or not.

In parliamentary systems, two parties compete in the electorate. The one getting a majority in parliament forms a government. Through cohesive voting on policy, the governing party is then in a position to pass its own program at will. Similarly, if the other party gains majority status in future would be able to pass its own program at will, which also means that if it wants to abolish everything the first party put in place. The classic parliamentary model, therefore, drastically heightens the dangers of political uncertainty. Worse, the governing party itself has full authority to renege at any time on any political deals it has second thoughts about. In a system of unchecked authority, then, there is no built-in protection for the legal status quo, and nothing to be gained from formalizing. Another property of parliamentary government is that the executive arises out of the legislature and both are controlled by the majority.

In a parliamentary democracy, elections to Parliament and lower houses of legislatures in the states decide the destiny of the current national and state administrations, respectively; ushering in new governments. Election is a mode not only for induction of office-bearers in a government but also the legislators. The electorate and political parties are the key variables in the electoral process, while election administration is the minor component. Together, these three variables form the triangle. Even so, the electoral process depends heavily on the role that the election administration plays. Immense significance of the elections to parliament, state legislatures, and executive positions is due to their authoritative and significant role in the formation and operation of governments, along with their influence on the lives of the people under their care. Elections invest the executive and legislative branches with the representative nature they need to reflect the will of the people.

In the democratic era, voting or suffrage in legislative and executive elections is considered a right or privilege of a citizen-referred as a 'normative'[14] or 'ethical'[15] role of the elections. When viewed from the perspective of the government, nonetheless it turns into the responsibility or function of the voter that elects the rulers to office- an 'instrumental'[16] role of the election phenomenon.

Outwardly process of elections seems to be fairly simple: people select from a list of names whom they wish to lead, the votes are counted, and the results are announced. However, the process is associated with many significant challenges. There are often powerful forces with an interest in the outcome of the elections with no hesitation against trying to win through irregular means. There are problems arising due to lack of infrastructure like ballots, ballot boxes, counting facilities, etc.; apathy among voters and deficient voter mobilization; lack of knowledge among voters regarding participation in elections; and, most importantly, questions surrounding freeness and fairness in the conduct of elections.

3. Evolution of Parliamentary Democratic Process in India

Elections in independent India are conceived to be both the commencement and culmination of the parliamentary democratic process in the country. The idea of parliamentary and electoral democracy was an exotic plant when it was conceived in colonial India. But once planted, it received sustenance and strength in the course of the national freedom movement in the country.[17] Thus, the foundation of parliamentary and electoral democracy has now deeply ingrained in Indian culture and customs as the soil and people of India.

The monarchical system was the foundation of ancient and medieval India. With the exception of the early Vedic era, the status of rulers in ancient India was based on inheritance. The Samitis and Sabhas were also aristocratic groups. The village councils, which comprised of village elders, were chosen by consensus as opposed to by election. It was only the British who introduced the representative institutions in India and the idea of elections. The right to vote was considered a privilege by the British government. It was believed that only a select few with privileges could exercise their right to vote, while others lacked the ability to use their right to vote in a manner that would be desirable. The only people deemed capable of responsibly casting ballots were those with a clear stake in agricultural land or a vocation. The Indian Councils Act, 1892, permitted the government to propose eminent individuals, who were mostly elected by local bodies, to the councils without giving up the right to a direct election. An elite special electorate made up of universities, landholders associations, chambers of commerce, and the like was created to augment the small electorate that was based on high property credentials.

Even more concerning than the privilege of representation was the communal bias ingrained in the 1909 Act. The Muslims were separated from the rest of the Indian population and granted voting rights on the basis of property credentials lower than those of their fellow Indians. The Government of India Acts of 1919 and 1935 essentially broke the democratic structure of the electorate by applying the communal divisions of the electorates to Muslims, Christians, Sikhs, Europeans, and others even within the Hindu fold. The franchise instituted by the 1919 Act, did not cover even 2.8 percent of the population. Only big landowners and tenants, and rich professionals were qualified for the vote, whereas the middle class, small peasantry and tenantry, women, and labour were denied the vote. Only a quarter of the literate were conferred the right to vote in the 1919 Act. The situation did not improve much under the Government of India Act, 1935. The government was content with the symbolic representation, and even the 1935 Act did not enfranchise more than 12 percent of the total population. It only added to the list of voters, a small additional percentage of women, industrial labour and depressed classes through supplementary qualifications. The tenants-at-will, landless labourers and hapless village craftsmen were still left out of the electoral roll.

Like their predecessors, the founding fathers of the Indian Constitution recognized free, regular, and secret elections to legislatures based on adult suffrage as a necessary component of democratic parliamentary government both at the Centre and state levels. The responsibility of the executive to Parliament (specifically, the popularly elected house) and of the representatives to the represented or constituency, which were the unique feature of the British government, also influenced and shaped the thinking of our Constitution-makers. Individual freedom and human equality served as the two ideological pillars of the theory of adult franchise. John Stuart Mill, whose ideas had a significant impact on Indian liberals' ideology, wrote:

> *"Men, as well as women, do not need political rights in order that they may govern, but in order that they may not be misgoverned. The majority of the male sex are, and will be all their lives, nothing else than labourers in corn-fields or manufactories; but this does not render the suffrage less desirable for them, nor their claim less to it, less irresistible, when not likely to make bad use of it. Nobody pretends to think that woman would make a bad use of the suffrage. The worst that is said is they would vote as mere dependents, at the bidding of their male relations. If it be so, so let it be. If they think for themselves, great good will be done, and if they do not, no harm. It is a benefit to human beings to take off their fetters, even if they do not desire to walk."*[18]

For Gandhiji franchise was a tool for self-defense and a means to regulate the relationship of a man with other members of society.[19] Thus framers of the constitution took four fundamental decisions –(i) conferment of the right to vote on all adults by the Constitution[20], (ii) abolition of the communal and special representation, which was rampant in the elections to the Legislatures under the British regime, (except in the case of the underdeveloped Scheduled Castes and Scheduled Tribes)[21] (SCs & STs), (iii) to have single member constituencies with simple majority system, with single non-transferable vote, except where seats were reserved for the SC & ST[22] and (iv) to establish an independent Election Commission with secured tenure to superintend, direct and control the preparation and conduct of elections to the Parliament and the State Legislatures.[23]

4. Constitutional Provisions to Elections

India, a Socialist, Secular, Democratic Republic, is the largest democracy in the World. The modern India, which came into existence on 15th of August 1947, is a constitutional democracy with a parliamentary system of government. At the heart of the system lies a commitment to hold regular, free and fair elections which determine the composition of the government, the membership of the two Houses of Parliament, the State and Union Territory Legislative Assemblies, and the Presidency and Vice-Presidency.

India has a written Constitution. The Indian Constitution has adopted a democratic republican form of government for the country and its salient provisions have been largely adopted with suitable modifications from the constitutions and constitutional practices of other democratic countries like the United Kingdom, the United States of America, Canada and Australia. The provisions dealing with conduct of elections in India are contained in the Constitution, supplemented by laws made by Parliament. The major laws governing elections are: Representation of the People Act, 1950- dealing with the preparation and revision of electoral rolls, and the Representation of the People Act, 1951, which in detail provides for all aspects of conduct of elections and post-election disputes.

4.1 Provisions relating to the Election of President

The President of India is elected by the Members of an Electoral College consisting of (a) the elected members of both Houses of Parliament and (b) the elected members of the Legislative Assemblies of the States. [24] For the purpose of this Article and Article 55 the state includes National Capital Territory of Delhi and the Union Territory of Puducherry.[25] The members nominated to either House of Parliament or the Legislative Assemblies of

States including NCT of Delhi and Union Territory of Puducherry are not eligible to be included in the Electoral College.

The Constitution mandates that there shall be uniformity, as far as practicable, in the scale of representation of the different States at the election.[26] To ensure such uniformity among the States inter-se as well as parity between the States as a whole and the Union, Constitution specifies a formula based on the population of each State for determination of the value of vote which each elected Member of Parliament and of the Legislative Assembly of each State is entitled to cast.

Every elected member of the Legislative Assembly of a State shall have as many votes as there are multiples of one thousand in the quotient obtained by dividing the population of the State by the total number of the elected members of the Assembly. If, after taking the said multiples of one thousand, the remainder is not less than five hundred, then the vote of each member shall be further increased by one.[27] Each elected member of either House of Parliament shall have such number of votes as may be obtained by dividing the total number of votes assigned to the members of the Legislative Assemblies of the States under sub-clauses (a) and (b) by the total number of the elected members of both Houses of Parliament, fractions exceeding one-half being counted as one and other fractions being disregarded.[28] Article 55(3) stipulates that the election of the President shall be held in accordance with the system of proportional representation by means of the single transferable vote and the voting at such election shall be by secret ballot. Proviso added to the Explanation by the Constitution (Eighty-fourth) Amendment Act, 2001 provides that until the relevant population figures for the first census to be taken after the year 2026 have been published, the population of the States for the purposes of calculation of value of votes for the Presidential Election shall mean the population as ascertained at the 1971-census.

A person who holds, or who has held, office as President shall be eligible for re-election to that office.[29] A person cannot be elected as President unless he—is a citizen of India, has completed the age of thirty-five years, and is qualified for election as a member of the House of the People.[30] A person is not be eligible for election as President if he holds any office of profit under the Government of India or the Government of any State or under any local or other authority subject to the control of any of the said Governments.[31]

4.2 Election of Vice-President

The Vice-President is elected by an electoral college consisting of members of both Houses of Parliament, in accordance with the system of proportional representation by means of the single transferable vote and the voting in such election is by secret ballot. The Electoral College to elect a person to the office of the Vice-President consists of all members of both Houses of Parliament. The Vice-President is not a member of either House of Parliament or of a House of a Legislature of any state. If a member of either House of Parliament or of a House of a Legislature of any state is elected as Vice-President, he is deemed to have vacated his seat in that House on the date he/she enters his office as Vice-President.[32] A person cannot be elected as Vice-President unless he -is a citizen of India; has completed the age of 35 years, and is qualified for election as a member of the Council of States (Rajya Sabha).[33] A person is not also eligible if he holds any office of profit under the Government of India or a State Government or any subordinate local authority.[34]

An election to fill a vacancy caused by the expiry of the term of office of Vice-President is completed before the expiry of the term. In case a vacancy arises by reasons of death, resignation or removal or otherwise, the election to fill that vacancy is held as soon as possible after the occurrence.[35] The person so elected is entitled to hold office for a full term of 5 years from the date he enters office.[36]

4.3 System of Election to Lok Sabha

The tenure of Lok Sabha, unless sooner dissolved, shall be for five years from the date appointed for its first meeting and no longer and the expiration of the said period of five years shall operate as a dissolution of the House. However, the said period may, while a Proclamation of Emergency is in operation, be extended by Parliament by law for a period not exceeding one year at a time and not extending in any case beyond a period of six months after the Proclamation has ceased to operate.[37]

Article 85 (2)(b) of the Constitution of India vests the President with the power to dissolve the House of the People. Similar power has been given the Governor of the State is provided under Article 174 (2)(b) of the Constitution for dissolution of State Legislative Assemblies. In the event of a State being under President's Rule as provided under Article 356, the

Legislative Assembly of the said State may be prematurely dissolved by the President.

Article 356 is pertinent in respect of premature dissolution of a State Legislative Assemblies. In case a State is brought under President's Rule as provided under Article 356, the Legislative Assembly of the said State may be prematurely dissolved by the President. In past, there have been several instances of proclamation of President's Rule in States under Article 356 wherein the State Assemblies were dissolved prematurely. In the light of Anti-Defection Act, 1985 and the judgement of the Supreme Court of India in *S.R. Bommai v. Union of India*[38] now the pre-mature dissolution of State Assemblies has been made significantly stringent. The constitutional bench of the apex court laid down guidelines for proclamation of President's Rule by the Union Government:

- The court reaffirming recommendation of the Sarkaria Commission held that even though Article 356 confers special powers on the President, such powers should be utilized by the President with great caution.
- No dissolution of assembly before Parliamentary approval- the proclamation issued by the President must be thoroughly analysed by both houses of the Parliament as per Article 356(3).
- In case the President issues the proclamation without the approval of both houses then the proclamation would lapse within a period of two months and the state assembly comes into force again.
- The proclamation under Article 356 is also subjected to judicial review. The High Court or the Supreme Court shall have the right to entertain a writ petition challenging the proclamation if it is satisfied that the writ petition raises question regarding the legality of the proclamation. If the situation requires, the court may also stop the President from dissolving the Legislative Assembly.
- The President's power to dismiss a state government is not absolute.

The elections to Lok Sabha and Vidhan Sabhas are conducted through the plurality system, or simple majority system, also known as the First Past the Post method. The candidate who receives the most votes in a constituency is deemed elected under this voting system. The candidate who finishes ahead of the competition and crosses the winning post first wins the election.

Article 81 (1) of the Constitution provides that the House of the People or Lok Sabha shall not have not more than 550 members of which 530 shall be chosen by direct election from territorial constituencies in the States and 20 members to represent the Union territories, elected in a manner as provided by Parliamentary law. At present Lok Sabha consists of 543 elected members, chosen directly from single member territorial Parliamentary constituencies.

For the purposes of elections, each State shall be allotted a number of seats in the House of the People in such manner that the ratio between that number and the population of the State remains almost same for all States.[39] Each State shall be divided into territorial constituencies in a way that the ratio between the population of each constituency and the number of seats allotted to it, as far as practicable, is same throughout the State.[40]

The expression "population" means the population as ascertained at the last preceding census of which the relevant figures have been published. The reference to the last preceding census of which the relevant figures have been published shall, until the relevant figures for the first census taken after the year 2026 have been published, shall be understood for the purposes of sub-clause (a) of clause (2) and the proviso to that clause, as a reference to the 1971 census; and (ii) for the purposes of sub-clause (b) of clause (2) as a reference to 2001 census.[41]

Article 82 provides that upon the completion of each census, the allocation of seats in the House of the People to the States and the division of each State into territorial constituencies shall be readjusted by such authority and in such manner as Parliament may by law determine. An Independent Delimitation Commission carries out the function of determining the size and shape of the parliamentary constituencies, and aims to create constituencies which have roughly the same population, subject to geographical considerations and the boundaries of the States. Delimitation is the process of redrawing of the boundaries of parliamentary or assembly constituencies to ensure that as far as practicable, there are same number of people in each constituency. This delimitation process is required to be carried out to examine the boundaries after ten-yearly census to reflect changes in population. For this, the Parliament by law establishes an Independent Delimitation Commission, which consists of the Chief Election

Commissioner and two judges or ex-judges from the Supreme Court or High Court. However, the delimitation was suspended until after the first census that takes place after the year 2026 by Constitution (Eighty-fourth Amendment) Act, 2001. Till then the allocation of seats in the House of the People and the State Assemblies may be readjusted on the basis of the 1971 census; and the division of each State into territorial constituencies be readjusted on the basis of the 2001 census.

4.4 Elections to Rajya Sabha

The composition of the upper House of Parliament, the Council of States, or Rajya Sabha has been provided in Article 80. Rajya Sabha shall consist of not more than 250 members, of which 12 are to be nominated by the President and 238 represent the States and Union territories. The members to be nominated by the President shall consist of persons having special knowledge or practical experience in respect of such matters as literature, science, art, and social service. The present strength of the Rajya Sabha is 245, out of which 233 are elected by the Vidhan Sabhas and 12 are nominated by the President. Rajya Sabha is a permanent body and not subject to dissolution.[42] Each member of Rajya Sabha is elected for a term of six years with one-third of its members retiring every second year, and are replaced by newly elected members. The elections to the Rajya Sabha are indirect; they are elected by each state Vidhan Sabha through a single transferable vote system. Elections are staggered, with one-third of its members getting elected every 2 years.

4.5 Elections to State Legislatures

India being a federal country, Constitution gives States and Union Territories significant control over their own government. For every State there shall be a Legislature. Where there are two Houses of the Legislature of a State, one shall be known as the Legislative Council and the other as the Legislative Assembly. However, where there is only one House, it shall be known as the Legislative Assembly. Out of 28 states, six, viz. Andhra Pradesh, Bihar, Karnataka, Maharashtra, Telangana, and Uttar Pradesh, have bicameral legislatures; the rest of the states have a unicameral legislature.

Every Legislative Assembly of every State, unless sooner dissolved, shall continue for five years from the date appointed for its first meeting and no longer and the expiration of the said period of five years shall operate as a dissolution of the Assembly. However, the said period may, while a Proclamation of Emergency is in operation, be extended by Parliament by law for a period not exceeding one year at a time and not extending in any case beyond a period of six months after the Proclamation has ceased to operate.[43] Legislative assemblies, or Vidhan Sabhas, are directly elected bodies; chosen by direct election from territorial constituencies in the state. The Legislative Assembly of each state shall not have more than 500, with at least sixty chosen by direct election from territorial constituencies in the state. Elections to the Vidhan Sabhas are conducted in a manner similar to that of the Lok Sabha; the first-past-the-post electoral system is used. The States and Union Territories are divided into single-member Assembly constituencies, which range in size, according to population. Uttar Pradesh has the largest legislature in India, its Legislative Assembly consists of 403 elected members. The smallest Vidhan Sabha is Puducherry, with 30 elected members.

4.6 Composition of the Legislative Councils

The Legislative Council of a State is not subject to dissolution. But as nearly as possible one-third of the members retire on the expiration of every second year in accordance with the provisions made in that behalf by Parliament by law.[44]

The total number of members in the Legislative Council shall not exceed one-third of the total number of members in the Legislative Assembly of that state. However, the total number of members in the Legislative Council of a State shall in no case be less than 40. The members of Vidhan Parishads are chosen by the members of the Vidhan Sabhas and local authorities, as well as by graduates and teachers in the state having such Parishads. Certain members are nominated by the Governor of the State to give representation to art, science, literature, social service, and cooperative movements. The elections to Vidhan Parishads are held according to the system of proportional representation by means of a single transferable vote.

4.7 Adult Suffrage

The elections to the Lok Sabha and to the Legislative Assembly of every State is on the basis of adult suffrage.[45] Any citizen of India over the age of 18 can vote in an election to Lok Sabha or Vidhan Sabha. Before 1989 the age of voting was 21. The right to vote is regardless of caste, creed, religion or gender. Those who are deemed to be of unsound mind, and people convicted of certain criminal offences are not allowed to vote.

5. Election Commission-Role and Functions

5.1 Election Commission

The management and conduct of elections on such large scale is humongous task and has inherent problems. Direct, free and fair elections are not only desirable but *sine qua non* to ensure political accountability and responsiveness.[46] Therefore, the Constitution entrusts the management and conduct of election on an independent body-Election Commission of India. The superintendence, direction and control of the preparation of the electoral rolls for, and the conduct of, all elections to Parliament and to the Legislature of every State and of elections to the offices of President and Vice-President have been entrusted to Election Commission.[47] The appointment of the Chief Election Commissioner and other Election Commissioners is made by the President. The Election Commission shall consist of the Chief Election Commissioner and such number of other Election Commissioners as the President may from time to time fix. The appointment of the Chief Election Commissioner and other Election Commissioners shall, be subject to the provisions of any law made in that behalf by Parliament.[48] In accordance with the provisions of the Constitution, the Election Commission was established on 25th January 1950. Originally, the commission had only a Chief Election Commissioner. with effect from 1st October, 1993, the Commission is a three- member body, consisting of Chief Election Commissioner and two Election Commissioners.

When any other Election Commissioner is so appointed, the Chief Election Commissioner shall act as the Chairman of the Commission. The conditions of service and tenure of office of the Election Commissioner and the Regional Commissioners shall be such as the President may by rule determine. They can be removed from office in like manner and on the like grounds as a Judge of the Supreme Court. The conditions of service of the Chief Election Commissioner shall not be varied to his disadvantage after his appointment. Any other Election Commissioner or a Regional Commissioner shall not be removed from office except on the recommendation of the Chief Election Commissioner.[49] The Chief and other Election Commissioners have tenure of six years, or up to the age of 65 years, whichever is earlier. They enjoy the same status and service conditions as are enjoyed by the Judges of the Supreme Court of India and can be removed from office only through impeachment by Parliament.

The President or the Governor of a state shall, when so requested by the Election Commission, make available to the Election Commissioner or to a Regional Commissioner such staff as may be necessary for the discharge of the functions conferred on the Election Commission.[50] Thus, the nature of appointment, the tenure security and the independence conferred on the Election Commission under the Constitution enables it to conduct its duties in a free and fair manner. However, it may be pointed out that mere constitutional status and the provisions to ensure its functioning, fairly and independently, will not serve the objective unless persons of calibre and competence are drawn to perform the task assigned. It is essential to maintain the neutral character of the Commission.

The main functions performed by the Election Commission are as follows:

1. Superintendence, etc., of the preparation of the electoral rolls for all the elections.
2. Appointing Chief Electoral Officers for each state, and Electoral Registration Officers for each constituency.
3. Granting recognition to Political parties and allot election symbols to them.
4. Conducting all elections.
5. Receiving election complaints.
6. Removing disqualification incurred for commission of corrupt practices during elections.
7. Deciding schedules of elections and by-elections and issuing notification for the same.
8. Advising the President on the question of disqualification of any member of Parliament.
9. Advising the Governor on the question of disqualification of the member of the State Legislature.

5.2 State Election Commission

Before 1992, elections to institutions of local self-government were conducted by the respective State Governments. The 73rd and 74th Constitutional amendments in 1992 inserted Part IX to adopt the new system of Panchayati Raj and Part IX A granting constitutional status to municipalities respectively. This also facilitated creation of State Election Commissions (SECs), constitutional bodies responsible for administering elections to the third tier of governance both in rural and urban areas (panchayati raj institutions, municipal bodies etc.). Article 243K and Article 243 ZA were inserted which provided for establishing a State Election Commission in every state as a constitutional body. Article 243K provides that the superintendence, direction and control of the preparation of electoral rolls for, and the conduct of, all elections to the Panchayats shall be vested in a State Election Commission consisting of a State Election Commissioner to be appointed by the Governor. Article 243ZA vests the superintendence, direction and control of the preparation of electoral rolls for, and the conduct of, all elections to the Municipalities in the State Election Commission referred to in Article 243K.

6. Reservation of seats

6.1 Reservation of seats in Lok Sabha

The Constitution provides for reservation of seats in the House of the People for — the Scheduled Castes; the Scheduled Tribes except the Scheduled Tribes in the autonomous districts of Assam; and the Scheduled Tribes in the autonomous districts of Assam.[51]

The number of seats reserved in any State or Union territory for the Scheduled Castes or the Scheduled Tribes shall bear the same proportion to the total number of seats allotted to that State or Union territory in the House of the People as the population of the Scheduled Castes in the State or Union territory or the Scheduled Tribes in the State or Union territory or part of the State or Union territory in respect of which seats are so reserved, bears to the total population of the State or Union territory.[52]

Article 330A providing for reservation of seats for women in the House of the People has been introduced in 2023 through Constitution (One Hundred and Sixth Amendment) Act, 2023. It provides that seats shall be reserved for women in the House of the People. Also one-third of the total number of seats reserved for SC/ST shall be reserved for women belonging to the Scheduled Castes or the Scheduled Tribes. One-third (including the number of seats reserved for women belonging to the Scheduled Castes and the Scheduled Tribes) of the total number of seats to be filled by direct election to the House of the People shall be reserved for women.

The President may, if he is of opinion that the Anglo-Indian community is not adequately represented in the House of the People, nominate not more than two members of that community to the House of the People.[53]

6.2 Reservation of seats in Vidhan Sabha

Seats shall be reserved for the Scheduled Castes and the Scheduled Tribes in the Legislative Assembly of every State. Seats shall be reserved also for the autonomous districts in the Legislative Assembly of the State of Assam. The number of seats reserved for the Scheduled Castes or the Scheduled Tribes in the Legislative Assembly of any State shall bear the same proportion to the total number of seats in the Assembly as the population of the Scheduled Castes in the State or of the Scheduled Tribes in the State or part of the State, in respect of which seats are so reserved, bears to the total population of the State.[54]

Article 332A inserted by Constitution (One Hundred and Sixth Amendment) Act, 2023 makes provision for Reservation of seats for women in the Legislative Assemblies of the States. Seats shall be reserved for women in the Legislative Assembly of every State. One-third of the total number of seats reserved for SC/ST shall be reserved for women belonging to the Scheduled Castes or the Scheduled Tribes. One-third (including the number of seats reserved for women belonging to the Scheduled Castes and the Scheduled Tribes) of the total number of seats to be filled by direct election in the Legislative Assembly of every State shall be reserved for women.

The Governor of a State may if he is of opinion that the Anglo-Indian community needs representation in the Legislative Assembly of the State and is not adequately represented therein, nominate one member of that community to the Assembly.[55]

The reservation of seats for the Scheduled Castes and the Scheduled Tribes in the House of the People and in the Legislative Assemblies of the States; and (b) the representation of the Anglo-Indian community in the House of the People and in the Legislative Assemblies of the States by nomination shall cease to have effect on the expiration of a period of 80 years in respect of clause (a) and 70 years in respect of clause (b) from the commencement of the Constitution. [56] The time limit for terminating SC and ST seats in the House of Commons and State Legislatures has been extended from 70 to 80 years by the 104th Amendment to the Indian Constitution. Whereas it has removed the seats reserved for the Anglo-Indian community in the Lok Sabha and the Vidhan Sabhas.

7. Elections for Local Self Government Institutions

7.1 Elections to Panchayati Raj Institutions

The Constitution 73rd Amendment Act, 1992 received the assent of the President on April 20, 1993 and was notified on April 24, 1993. As per the amendment, Part IX on the Panchayats has been inserted to the Constitution and the states have be constitutionally mandated to establish Panchayats and bestow them with power and functions. Important aspects of Part IX of the Constitution are as follows:

Constitution of Panchayats

"**Panchayat**" means an institution (by whatever name called) of self government constituted under Article 243B, for the rural areas.[57] There shall be constituted in every State, Panchayats at the village, intermediate and district levels in accordance with the provisions of this Part.[58] Notwithstanding anything in Clause (1), Panchayats at the intermediate level may not be constituted in a State having a population not exceeding twenty lakhs.[59]

Gram Sabha-"Gram Sabha" means a body consisting of persons registered in the electoral rolls relating to a village comprised within the area of Panchayat at the village level;[60] A Gram Sabha may exercise such powers and perform such functions at the village level as the Legislature of a State may, by law, provide.[61]

Composition of Panchayats

Article 243C of the Constitution provides for the Composition of the Panchayats. The Legislature of a State may, by law, make provisions with respect to the composition of Panchayats. However, the ratio between the population of the territorial area of a Panchayat at any level and the number of seats in such Panchayat to be filled by election shall, so far as practicable, be the same throughout the State. All the seats in a Panchayat shall be filled by persons chosen by direct election from territorial constituencies in the Panchayat area and, for this purpose, each Panchayat area shall be divided into territorial constituencies in such manner that the ratio between the population of each constituency and the number of seats allotted to it shall, so far as practicable, be the same throughout the Panchayat area.

The Legislature of a State may, by law, provide for the representation –

a. of the Chairpersons of the Panchayats at the village level, in the Panchayats at the intermediate level or, in the case of a State not having Panchayats at the intermediate level, in the Panchayats at the district level;

b. of the Chairpersons of the Panchayats at the intermediate level, in the Panchayats at the district level;

c. of the members of the House of the People and the Members of the Legislative Assembly of the State representing constituencies which comprise wholly or partly Panchayat area at a level other than the village level, in such Panchayat;

d. of the members of the Council of States and the members of the Legislative Council of the State, where they are registered as electors within - i. a Panchayat area at the intermediate level, in Panchayat at the intermediate level; ii. a Panchayat area at the district level, in Panchayat at the district level.

The Chairperson of a Panchayat and other members of a Panchayat whether or not chosen by direct election from territorial constituencies in the Panchayat area shall have the right to vote in the meetings of the Panchayats.

Reservation of Seats

Article 243D provides for Reservation of seats at panchayat level it provides that seats shall be reserved for –

a. the Scheduled Castes; and

b. the Scheduled Tribes,

in every Panchayat and the number of seats so reserved shall bear, as nearly as may be, the same proportion to the total number of seats to be filled by direct election in that Panchayat as the population of the Scheduled Castes in that Panchayat area or of the Scheduled Tribes in that Panchayat area bears to the total population of that area and such seats may be allotted by rotation to different constituencies in a Panchayat.[62]

Reservation for Women-Not less than one-third of the total number of seats reserved under clause (1) shall be reserved for women belonging to the Scheduled Castes or, as the case may be, the Scheduled Tribes.

Not less than one-third (including the number of seats reserved for women belonging to the Scheduled Castes and the Scheduled Tribes) of the total number of seats to be filled by direct election in every Panchayat shall be reserved for women and such seats may be allotted by rotation to different constituencies in a Panchayat.[63]

Reservation to the offices of the Chairperson- The offices of the Chairpersons in the Panchayats at the village or any other level shall be reserved for the Scheduled Castes, the Scheduled Tribes and women in such manner as the Legislature of a State may, by law, provide. However, the number of offices of Chairpersons reserved for the Scheduled Castes and the Scheduled Tribes in the Panchayats at each level in any State shall bear, as nearly as may be, the same proportion to the total number of such offices in the Panchayats at each level as the population of the Scheduled Castes in the State or of the Scheduled Tribes in the State bears to the total population of the State. Not less than one-third of the total number of offices of Chairpersons in the Panchayats at each level shall be reserved for women. The number of offices reserved under this clause shall be allotted by rotation to different Panchayats at each level.

Duration of Panchayats

Every Panchayat, unless sooner dissolved under any law for the time being in force, shall continue for five years from the date appointed for its first meeting and no longer.[64]

An election to constitute a Panchayat shall be completed - a. before the expiry of its duration specified in clause (1); b. before the expiration of a period of six months from the date of its dissolution. Provided that where the remainder of the period for which the dissolved Panchayat would have continued is less than six months, it shall not be necessary to hold any election under this clause for constituting the Panchayat. A Panchayat constituted upon the dissolution of a Panchayat before the expiration of its duration shall continue only for the remainder of the period for which the dissolved Panchayat would have continued under Clause (1) had it not been so dissolved.[65]

7.2 Elections for Municipalities

Constitution (Seventy Forth Amendment) Act, 1992 and Municipalities

Constitution (Seventy Forth Amendment) Act, 1992 has introduced a new Part IXA in the Constitution, which deals with Municipalities in an Articles 243 P to 243 ZG. This amendment, also known as Nagarpalika Act, came into force on 1st June 1993. It has given constitutional status to the municipalities and brought them under the justifiable part of the Constitution. States were put under constitutional obligation to adopt municipalities as per system enshrined in the Constitution.

Article 243P of the Constitution provides definitions of important concepts.

e) **"Municipality"** means an institution of self-government constituted under article 243Q;

(c) **"Metropolitan area"** means an area having a population of ten lakhs or more, comprised in one or more districts and consisting of two or more Municipalities or Panchayats or other contiguous areas, specified by the Governor by public notification to be a Metropolitan area for the purposes of this Part;

(d) **"Municipal area"** means the territorial area of a Municipality as is notified by the Governor;

(a) **"Committee"** means a Committee constituted under Article 243S;

Kinds of Municipalities

Article 243Q provides for establishment of 3 kinds of Municipalities in every state.

(a) a Nagar Panchayat (by whatever name called) for a transitional area, that is to say, an area in transition from a rural area to an urban area;

(b) a Municipal Council for a smaller urban area; and

(c) a Municipal Corporation for a larger urban area,

Provided that a Municipality under this clause may not be constituted in such urban area or part thereof as the Governor may, having regard to the size of the area and the municipal services being provided or proposed to be provided by an industrial establishment in that area and such other factors as he may deem fit, by public notification, specify to be an industrial township.

In this Article, "a transitional area", "a smaller urban area" or "a larger urban area" means such area as the Governor may, having regard to the population of the area, the density of the population therein, the revenue generated for local administration, the percentage of employment in non-agricultural activities, the economic importance or such other factors as he may deem fit, specify by public notification for the purposes of this Part.

Composition of Municipalities

Article 243R provides that all the seats in a Municipality shall be filled by persons chosen by direct election from the territorial constituencies in the Municipal area and for this purpose each Municipal area shall be divided into territorial constituencies to be known as wards. The Legislature of a State may, by law, provide— (a) for the representation in a Municipality of—

(i) persons having special knowledge or experience in Municipal administration;

(ii) the members of the House of the People and the members of the Legislative Assembly of the State representing constituencies which comprise wholly or partly the Municipal area;

(iii) the members of the Council of States and the members of the Legislative Council of the State registered as electors within the Municipal area;

(iv) the Chairpersons of the Committees constituted under clause (5) of article 243S.

Reservation of Seats

Seats shall be reserved for the Scheduled Castes and the Scheduled Tribes in every Municipality and the number of seats so reserved shall bear, as nearly as may be, the same proportion to the total number of seats to be filled by direct election in that Municipality as the population of the Scheduled Castes in the Municipal area or of the Scheduled Tribes in the Municipal area bears to the total population of that area and such seats may be allotted by rotation to different constituencies in a Municipality.[66]

Not less than one-third of the total number of seats reserved under clause (1) shall be reserved for women belonging to the Scheduled Castes or, as the case may be, the Scheduled Tribes.[67]

Not less than one-third (including the number of seats reserved for women belonging to the Scheduled Castes and the Scheduled Tribes) of the total number of seats to be filled by direct election in every Municipality shall be reserved for women and such seats may be allotted by rotation to different constituencies in a Municipality.[68] The offices of Chairpersons in the Municipalities shall be reserved for the Scheduled Castes, the Scheduled Tribes and women in such manner as the Legislature of a State may, by law, provide.[69]

Duration of Municipalities

Duration of the municipality has been fixed at 5 years from the date appointed for its first meeting. Elections to constitute a municipality are required to be completed before the expiration of the duration of the municipality. If the municipality is dissolved before the expiry of 5 years, the elections for constituting a new municipality are required to be completed within a period of 6 months from the date of its dissolution.[70]

8. Laws dealing with Elections

The Representation of the People Act ,1950

The Act provides for the allocation of seats in and the limitation of constituencies for the purpose of election to, the House of the People and the Legislatures of States, the qualifications of voters at such elections, the preparation of electoral rolls (the manner of filling seats in the Council of States to be filled by representatives of (Union Territories) and matters connected therewith.

The Registration of Electors Rules, 1960

These Rules have been formulated by the Central Government along with the Election Commission in exercise of powers under Section 28 of the Representation of the People Act, 1950. The rules provide the details for the preparation of electoral rolls, and their periodic updating and revision. The rules provide the procedure for the registration of eligible electors and the issue of voter ID cards or electoral identity cards with the voter's photograph. These also include rules on the inclusion of eligible voters, the exclusion of ineligible voters and any corrections required. These rules, thus empower the Election Commission to prepare the photo electoral rolls which will contain the name, photograph and other particulars of the electors.

The Representation of the People Act, 1951

The Act provides for the conduct of elections to the Houses of Parliament and to the House or Houses of the Legislatures of each state, the qualifications and disqualifications for membership of those Houses, the corrupt practices and other offences at or in connection with such elections and the decisions on doubts and disputes arising out of or in connection with such elections. According to the Act, all doubts and disputes arising out of the elections or in connection with the elections, will be dealt with in accordance to the provisions of this Act. All disputes can be raised in the High Court of the respective State. These post-election matters can be raised after the election is over and not during the process of it.

The Conduct of Elections Rules, 1961

The Conduct of Elections Rules, 1961 have been framed by the Central Government along with the Election Commission under Section 169 of the Act. These provide the detailed rules for every stage of the conduct of elections; incorporating the issue of the writ notification for conducting elections, filing of nominations, and the scrutiny of the nominations. It also deals with withdrawal of nominations by the candidates. Taking the polls and counting votes are also governed by these rules. Finally, the constitution of the Houses based on the results is also provided under these rules.

Model Code of Conduct (MCC)

The Model Code of Conduct (MCC) is a set of norms that prescribes several do's and do not's that political parties, contesting candidates, party(ies) in power have to strictly abide by during the process of elections. The MCC has been developed with the consent of political parties who have agreed to abide by its principles and to respect and observe it in its letter and spirit. The purpose of Model Code of Conduct is to ensure fair elections for all parties involved and a level playing field throughout the elections. It also provides for rules against the misuse of official machinery and power by the ruling party to maintain fairness in elections.

9.One Nation, One Election

9.1 Simultaneous Elections – Meaning and Scope

Federal democracies, which are frequently distinguished by the coexistence of national and subnational governmental levels, face a unique challenge-frequency of elections. In the past decades, India is also grappling with the same issue with hundreds of state assembly elections taking place. These frequent elections come at a high cost in terms of money and administrative work and also causing inconvenience to citizens, political parties and government. This has triggered a debate for adoption of 'One Nation, One Election' – simultaneous elections.

There is no specific definition of the term simultaneous election. Several terminological definitions of Simultaneous General Elections have been provided by experts. Sugato Dasgupta et al., describe "Simultaneous General Elections as General Elections that are held at the same time for several types of elections at once".[71] Shugart presents a refined opinion. According to him, "Simultaneous General Elections are general elections conducted at the same time to elect office holders at the national and regional levels, related to parliamentary candidates and presidential candidates for countries with a presidential system of government".[72] On basis of these definitions, it can be concluded that simultaneous general elections contain several different elections at once, both different in scope and positions filled.[73]

9.2 Models of Simultaneous General Elections

There is no uniform model for Simultaneous elections. Schakel and Dandoy based on their research among European countries, sampled countries which generally use parliamentary system of government, discovered the trends in the form of simultaneous elections conducted in the European region.[74] These trends have been grouped into six types of simultaneous election models, which are as follows:

(i) National, Provincial, and District/City simultaneity

In this model, all types of elections, both at the national and regional (provincial and district/city) levels, in a country are conducted simultaneously on the same day. These elections cover all levels, from the national to the regional level, both provincial and district/city. If the country adheres to the Presidential System of Government, the election of

Candidates for Members of the House of Representatives as power holders and Candidates for President - Vice President are conducted simultaneously. There are no other elections.

(ii) National and provincial simultaneity

In this concurrent model, elections in all provinces are conducted simultaneously with national elections on the same polling day. However, the elections at district level are conducted separately.

(iii) Provincial and district/city simultaneity

This simultaneous model focuses on organizing regional-level elections, simultaneously nationally. This simultaneous means that all general elections at the regional level (both provinces and district/city) are held on the same day. Meanwhile, general elections at the national level are held at different time, separate from general elections at the regional level.

(iv) Provincial simultaneity

In this model, all elections at the provincial level, both the election of legislative candidates and candidates for governor as the holder of executive power, are conducted simultaneously at the national level. In this model, elections at the national level as well as at the district/city level are conducted on other election days.

(v) Regency/City simultaneity

In this Model, simultaneity is only found in General Elections at the Regency /City level. The elections are held simultaneously for all regencies/cities in a province only. This model has implications for the implementation of different general elections in each province. Also, the timing of implementing general elections at the national and provincial levels is different.

(vi) Another simultaneity

Using a sample of EU member states, the Simultaneous Elections model is intended to classify countries that conduct elections for the President and Members of the EU Parliament on the same election day. Furthermore, the model is also used to classify countries that hold referendums simultaneously on the same day.

Besides, the studies which examined the models of simultaneous elections applicable in countries in Europe that generally adhere to the parliamentary system, there are also studies on models of simultaneous elections, which are compiled based on the results of research on countries in the Americas, including Latin America which generally use a presidential system of government. According to Syamsuddin Haris et al., models of simultaneous general elections consist of several types, among others.[75]

(i) National, Provincial, and District/City simultaneity

In this model of election, all elections are held at the same time. These elections cover all levels, from the national to the regional level, both provincial and district/city. Besides, the elections target more than just elections to fill the positions of members of parliament or heads of government. The elections include all holders of executive and legislative power.

(ii) Branches of Power Simultaneity

There are two stages of elections in this simultaneous model- general elections to fill the legislative branch of power and general elections to fill the executive branch of power. First legislative elections at the national and regional (provincial and district/city) levels would be held. The executive elections to elect the President as head of government at the national level along with regional heads across the country would be held sometime later simultaneously.

(iii) Levels of Government Simultaneity

The implementation of general elections is divided based on the level of government of a country in this simultaneous model. General elections are divided into two types: national general elections and regional general elections. Elections for members of the national parliament and the President are conducted simultaneously in national elections. Whereas, elections for regional heads and regional parliamentarians are conducted in regional elections.

(iv) Time Interval Based Simultaneity

In principle, this model of simultaneous elections is the same as the model based on simultaneous levels of government. However, there are important differences between the two regarding implementation time. In the simultaneous general election model of the concurrent levels of government, regional-level elections are conducted simultaneously in all regions. Meanwhile, this simultaneous model does not require the implementation of regional-level elections at one time only. Regional-level elections will be conducted periodically, such as in different islands or provinces, according to their geographical location. For example, the National General Election will be held in 2023, followed by the Regional General Election in 2024 for provinces located on Island A and the Regional General Election in 2024 for provinces located on Island B. With this kind of simultaneous model, general elections will continue to exist yearly.

(v) Flexible Provincial Simultaneity

The simultaneous election model is the same as the time interval-based simultaneous model. This model allows each provincial-level region to have different or the same general election time. This condition can occur because the simultaneity of local-level elections only covers the territory of a province. Provinces have the freedom/autonomy to determine when elections will be held in their provinces to elect members of parliament and regional heads, both at the provincial and district/city levels.

(vi) Legislative and Executive National Simultaneity

Unlike the previous models of simultaneous elections, which were structured based on levels of government and the division of branches of power, this model combines both. This model will elect members of parliament, both at the national and regional levels (provincial and district/city), simultaneously with the election of the President as the holder of executive power at the national level. Meanwhile, regional head elections are conducted simultaneously in all country regions.

9.3 Concurrent Elections-Country Specific Experience

(i) South Africa

In South Africa, national and provincial elections are held every five years. The electoral system for Parliament and Provincial assemblies is based on "proportional representation and party lists". Before the election, each political party provides a list of candidates arranged in numbered order of preference. The seats of Parliament are allocated in proportion to the number of votes cast in the election. This means a party that won 10% of the votes gets 10% of the seats. If a party wins 20 seats, the first 20 people on its party list become MPs.[76] The Independent Electoral Commission (IEC) established under the IEC Act, 1996 decides how many people from each party-list should take up seats in the legislatures. For Municipal Councils also elections are held after every five years though not along with National and Provincial elections. there is a "mixed-member system" in which, wards elect individual councillors alongside those named from party-lists.

(ii) Sweden

Sweden is a parliamentary democracy, there are no presidential elections in Sweden, only parliamentary elections. Sweden follows the proportional electoral system. The political parties are assigned number of seats in the elected assembly based on their share of votes. In their system elections for the Parliament (Riksdag), County Councils and Municipal Councils all take place at the same time. These elections occur every four years on the second Sunday of September whereas elections to the Municipal Assemblies occur on the second Sunday of September, once every five years. After an election, the Election Authority distributes the seats proportionally, depending on the number of votes that each party has received.[77]

(iii) Belgium

In Belgium, one can vote in five different elections:

- European elections: representatives for the European Parliament;
- Federal elections: for the federal parliament (the Chamber of Representatives);
- Regional elections: for the legislative bodies of the federated regions, e.g.: the Flemish Parliament, the Walloon Parliament, the Parliament of the Brussels Capital Region, the Parliament of the German-speaking Community;
- Provincial elections: for the Provincial council; and
- Municipal elections: for the Municipal council.

Elections for the Federal Parliament are normally held every five years, coinciding with the European (and consequently also regional) elections. The German Parliament can propose a resolution to remove the government only if it names a successor.

(iv) Indonesia

The Constitutional Court of Indonesia, while reviewing Law No. 42 Year 2008 concerning Presidential Elections, vide decision No.14/PUU-XI/2013, held that Indonesia will hold the presidential elections and legislative elections concurrently starting 2019, on the ground that Law

No.42 of 2008 was contrary to the constitutional provision. For India, Indonesia is a living laboratory to study the One-Nation, One-Election system, though their electorate is only about a quarter of India's. On 14th February, 2024, Indonesia successfully conducted simultaneous elections, being termed as the world's largest single day elections; wherein Indonesians chose a new president and vice president, a parliament, and lawmakers among 20,000 administrative posts across the country. Each voter on five ballot papers chose their preferred presidential and vice-presidential pairing, lawmakers at the national, provincial, and regency level, and a regional senator to advise the national parliament.

(v) Germany

German model of 'constructive no-confidence' stipulates that the unseating of a government must immediately be followed by the formation of a new one, which will serve out the remainder of the legislative term. Under the provisions of Basic Law of Germany, the only option for the Bundestag is to express its disapproval for the Government leader, by passing the motion containing the name of his successor (Art.67). This should be supported by majority of Deputies. If the motion is passed successfully then the Cabinet has to resign.

Simultaneous elections, in one form or the other, do exist in various parts of the world. Countries like Philippines, Brazil, Bolivia, Columbia, Costa Rica, Guatemala, Guyana, Honduras, Nicaragua et al, follow a system of simultaneous elections. However, these countries follow Presidential form of Government and the election of President and the elections to the Legislative are held together.

(vi) Philippines

The Philippines has a Presidential form of government. The country follows a system of simultaneous elections, by virtue of an Act passed in 1992 that paved the way for synchronized elections. In Philippines national and local elections are held simultaneously since 1995. Simultaneous elections are held for national and local officials at an interval of every three years. Section 3 of the 1992 Act specified that the term of President, Vice President, and Senators will be six years. Out of the twenty-four Senators elected in May 1992, the first twelve with the highest number of votes will serve for six years, and that the remaining twelve will serve for three years. Members of the House of Representatives and all elective provincial, city, and Municipal officials once elected will serve for a term of three years. Section 4 of the Act provides for full synchronisation of elections for President and Vice President on the second Monday of May and on the same day every six years thereafter. For the senators, all members of the House of Representatives and Municipal Officials, elections are held on the second Monday of May and on the same day every three years thereafter.

9.4 Simultaneous Election –Indian Scenario

India, the world's largest democracy, has over 968 million eligible voters. The country holds elections for multiple tiers of government, including the Lok Sabha, Rajya Sabha, state legislative assemblies, and local bodies. The foundation of India's electoral system is rooted in its Constitution, which outlines a federal structure, clearly dividing powers between the central and state governments. Over time, several high-level committees have reviewed potential electoral reforms such as public funding of elections, the right to recall legislators, and transitioning from the first-past-the-post system to proportional representation. Among these, the 'One Nation, One Election' proposal, which seeks to synchronize the election cycles of central and state governments, has sparked the most debate, aiming to streamline governance and reduce the cost and frequency of elections.

On September 18, 2024, the Union Cabinet, chaired by the Prime Minister Shri Narendra Modi, accepted the recommendations of the High-Level Committee on Simultaneous Elections under the chairmanship of former President Shri Ram Nath Kovind.[78] The simultaneous elections will be implemented in two phases. In first phase the elections to Lok Sabha and Assembly will be conducted simultaneously. In the second phase, the elections of the local body elections (panchayat and municipalities) will be conducted within 100 days of general elections. To implement the concurrent elections, common electoral roll for all elections will be prepared. The government will initiate detailed discussions throughout the country and also constitute an implementation group. The government proposes to bring three Bills in Parliament to implement simultaneous election. Out of these, two Bills include amending the Constitution to put in place the government's plan to hold simultaneous elections for the Lok Sabha, state assemblies and local bodies in a phased manner.[79]

In common parlance, "simultaneous elections" means conducting elections simultaneously for all three tiers of the constitutional institutions: the House of the People (Lok Sabha), State Assemblies (Vidhan Sabha), and local bodies. This essentially means that votes are cast on the same day to elect representatives at all three tier of government.[80]

Debates surrounding electoral expenditure, particularly the costs incurred in deploying personnel and the extended duration of the Model Code of Conduct, are critical in shaping the discourse on electoral reforms in India. The frequent conduct of elections not only adds financial strain but also amplifies caste, religious, and communal tensions, influencing social cohesion. These concerns fuel discussions on the feasibility of the 'One Nation, One Election' proposal, which seeks to reduce the frequency and associated challenges of conducting separate elections. In this document, we will explore these issues in detail, examining their implications for electoral efficiency and national unity.

The number of institutions at the third tier of governance is too large. As of April 2024, there are around 2.63 lakh panchayats in India.[81] The conduct of election to these institutions is a State subject. According to the Constitution, the elections to the third tier institutions are controlled and organized by their respective State Election Commissions. Therefore, synchronizing and aligning election schedules of all three tiers is difficult. Therefore, what 'One Nation, One Elections' contemplate is that that the elections of the House of the People and State Legislative Assemblies are conducted simultaneously—all electorates will vote in Lok Sabha and Assembly elections—to elect central and state representatives, in the same year, if not at the same time.

The Indian general elections 2024 were held by the Election Commission over the period April-June 2024 to constitute the 18th Lok Sabha. Along with elections to the Lok Sabha, elections for constituting the State Assemblies of only 3 states were held, which were Andhra Pradesh, Sikkim, and Odisha. The rest of the states followed a non-synced five-year cycle. Karnataka, Madhya Pradesh, Rajasthan, and Telangana, were among those voting at different times in the previous year, 2023. Haryana voted on October 5, 2024. The Union Territory of Jammu and Kashmir also held its first Assembly election after 10 years during September-October, 2024. Jharkhand, and Maharashtra will go for elections later this year. These will be followed by elections in Delhi, Bihar, West Bengal and Uttar Pradesh early next year.

These elections to State Assemblies were announced within two months of concluding the Lok Sabha elections and elections to other State Assemblies.

India is going for elections every six months, may it be state assemblies, elections to the third tier of Government (Panchayati Raj institutions / Municipal bodies), bye-elections, etc. The result is that the number of elections in any given year would substantially increase, putting a lot of pressure on resources. Regular elections have a detrimental effect on overall governing process and the administrative and development initiatives. Therefore, various stakeholders have expressed an urgent need to develop a mechanism to put an end to these recurrent election cycles. One potential solution being examined is holding simultaneous elections.

On examining the history of elections in India, one finds that general elections for the House of the People and State Legislative Assemblies were conducted simultaneously during the first two decades after independence, i.e., in the years 1951–1952, 1957, 1962, and 1967. During the first general elections held between October 1951 and May 1952, a three-tiered process was followed for electing the President and Vice-President, members of the Lower Houses at the Centre and in the States, and members of the Upper Houses. The main reason behind the synchronized elections till then was the dominance and rule by one national political party and the regional parties were not powerful and influential. The indiscriminate use of Article 356 of the Constitution also contributed to disruptions of simultaneous elections.

The Report on the Second General Elections in India, 1957 states:

> *"If the House of the People and the different State Legislative Assemblies were all allowed to complete their respective terms in full, the General elections to reconstitute them would have had to be held at different points of time. In such a case, it would not have been possible to hold simultaneous country-wide general elections, both for the House of the People and the State Legislative Assemblies.... It was therefore, decided that the second general elections should be completed before the end of March, 1957, and that the existing Houses of Legislature should be dissolved prematurely, whenever necessary, in order that the newly elected Houses might meet soon after the general elections were over."*[32]

In furtherance of this decision, seven State Legislative Assemblies Bihar, Bombay, Madras, Mysore, Punjab, Uttar Pradesh and West Bengal were dissolved prematurely. The decision to dissolve the Houses by the Election Commission of India was reached through consensual approach in consultation with all political parties, the Central Government and the State Governments. For the same the Election Commission called a conference of the All-India Political Parties in New Delhi on the 13th November, 1956.[83] The concurrent elections offered convenience for both the voters and the authorities responsible for the conduct of elections. Political parties and their candidates were also benefited.

9.5 The First Four General Elections after Independence-Brief

(i) 1951-52 - First General Elections in Independent India

The first general elections in independent India, under the Constitution of the India, were held in 1951-52. It certainly was the largest election ever held, "the biggest experiment in democracy in human history".[84] India took the decision to introduce universal suffrage in a country where 85 percent of the adult population was illiterate and poor; no less than 176 million persons were eligible to vote. Being the first elections in the independent India, it was expected that a large majority of them will go to the polls and most of them had never voted before. The elections were held for about 4500 seats in the House of the People in the Parliament and the State Legislative Assemblies, that too concurrently. Seven hundred million ballot papers were printed. Approximately 224,000 polling booths were constructed and equipped with over two million steel ballot boxes for smooth conduct of elections. Some 56,000 Presiding Officers for polling booths were required who were assisted by 280,000 clerks and 224,000 policemen. Atleast two million people actively participated in the conduct of the elections, either as officials or as political workers. The cost of conducting the elections for the central and state governments alone was estimated at more than $20 million;[85] the costs to the parties and candidates combined were even larger.

Being the first election for a country, which has undergone partition resulting in population transfer of unprecedented magnitude accompanied by devastating communal violence, the registration procedure for elections itself was a herculean task. Preparation of electoral rolls was even more tedious and difficult for India as compared to any other country because of the illiteracy of many citizens and thus the great difficulty was of getting names recorded properly. In addition, the large number of refugees in the country made necessary the special rule[86]. that only persons of 21 years of age or older on March 1, 1950 who have lived for at least 180 days in a constituency between April 1, 1947 and December 31, 1949 would have a right to vote in that constituency. Though the effect of this rule was to eliminate a moderate number of persons from the electoral rolls; but without such a rule, those compiling the official lists would have faced with the impossible job of deciding the formal residence of a shifting population. Nearly half of the potential voters were women; large number of whom, almost three million, refused to give their own names to the registration officers. They chose to be enrolled simply as wives or daughters, using the name of a male relative for the purpose of registration. The Election Commission ruled these registrations off the records; hoping that when the electoral rolls were revised in 1952 these women would understand the necessity for all citizens, regardless of sex, to take an individual part in the process of elections.

In the delimitation process, the constituencies for the House of the People were demarcated on contiguous-area basis, bearing in mind the constitutional provision that the population in each constituency shall range between 500,000 and 750,000. For this election, the number of persons per constituency was around 720,000. Thus in single-member constituencies each member of the House of the People represented over 700,000 persons. In the House of the People and in most of the State Legislative Assemblies, some seats were reserved for the Scheduled Tribes and the Scheduled Castes as per Constitutional mandate.

The Election Commission Report on the First General Elections[87] states "The conduct of elections in as large a country as India, among a still mainly illiterate population, where transport and communication are frequently difficult, is a very great administrative task." According to Richard Leonard Park[88], the 1951-52 general elections were experimental in nature. The electorate were enormous and politically inexperienced, and there are few precedents to guide observers. Nevertheless, the Government of India, the Election Commission, and the organized political parties of India earnestly attempted to make their first general election a fair and fruitful experiment in the development of a democratic India.

(ii) Second General Elections in 1957

The second national elections[89] since independence in India were held this year 1957 from February 24 to March 14. In these elections, over 115 million voters (nearly 60 percent of the 193 million eligible) casted their ballots for 488 members of Lok Sabha and for 2,901 members of the Vidhan Sabhas of 13 state assemblies, and for councils in two Union Territories. The elections were contested by over 50 political parties and an uncounted number of independents- according to one of the estimate, the total running for office at more than 14,000. Most of these parties were of local, and frequently temporary. Only 15 parties were given official recognition by the Election Commission. Four of these were recognized as "national" parties: Congress, Praja-Socialist, Communist, and Jana Sangh. The remaining were recognized as "state" parties. During this election some 200,000 polling station operated throughout the country, and the election was completed in less than three weeks and the results were announced by April 1. Indelible ink, 2,875,000 steel, tamper-proof ballot boxes, over 500 million ballot papers were used in the second general election.

(iii) 1962- Third General Elections

Nearly 114,000,000 voters took part in India's third general elections since independence which took place in February 1962.[90] Through these elections a new parliament was elected along with thirteen state assemblies.

(iv) Fourth General Elections in 1967

The changes in the political scenario could be sensed after the fourth General Elections held in 1967.[91] The dominance which the Congress Party had maintained for 20 years was broken. The key leaders including the party president, Shri K. Kamaraj, were defeated. In eight states (governing two-thirds of the Indian population) non-Congress governments were formed. Congress seats in the Lok Sahba dropped from 73.1% to 54.6%- with a loss of 81 seats. In elections to the Lok Sabha the Swatantra and Jana Sangh parties made striking gains in number of seats (from 18 and 12 in 1962 to 44 and 35 in 1967, respectively) with a relatively small increase in percentage of the popular vote.

The election witnessed the rise of stronger non-Congress parties and new party coalitions at the national as well as at the state level. If we examine 1967 elections in relation to 1962 elections, there are certain obvious phenomena which are visible. Firstly, there was allegiance and loyalty for both Congress and non-Congress partisans. Secondly, there was defection of 1962 voters/supporters from Congress to non-Congress parties and vice versa. On one hand the disinterest and withdrawal of 1962 voters was visible and on the other the involvement of new voters, both those eligible to vote in 1962 but who stayed home, and those eligible for the first time in 1967 could be seen. These changes in political dynamics in 1967 paved ways for prospective changes and probabilities of major political realignment in the future. In the 1967 elections, predominant movement was consistently away from Congress. If one compares the Lok Sabha -and state assembly votes which switched to Congress and away from Congress-the proportions are 29% to 71% against Congress. But the votes which switched away from Congress were so evenly distributed among the Right, the Left and the other parties that the disadvantage to Congress in gross terms was minimized.

The following are some of the aspects which emerged during the fourth general elections which not only changed the national political scenario but also resulted in elections becoming asynchronized afterwards:

The Congress monolith, which for so long has dominated the Indian political landscape, has been badly cracked, but not shattered.[92] The one party dominance, was no longer an accurate description of the party structure. Further the one party dominance was not succeeded by a two-party or three-party or multiple-party system, but rather, by "a cross-party polity of dubious value."[93] Even though in the fourth general elections Congress still emerged as the most important party; but this time its losses in seats in the Lok Sabha and the State Assemblies was even greater than the marked decline in its popular vote. On the fourth general elections, Eric da Costa, Director of the Indian Institute of Public Opinion, wrote:

> *The Indian electorate, believed inert and incapable of dramatic choice, is showing signs of a revolutionary change. The young, the less educated, and particularly illiterates, the minorities and, most unpredictable of all, the lowest income groups are all rewriting their basic loyalties. To the candidates this is, perhaps, a struggle for power. To a political scientist it is, as nearly half a century ago, the beginning of a break with the past.*[94]

The Congress failed to tackle grave national problems vigorously and to put its own house in order. It could not identify itself more realistically with the felt needs and aspirations of an increasingly conscious and increasingly demanding Indian electorate. After nearly twenty years of rule, it seemed vulnerable on many counts for its real or alleged sins of omission and commission.[95] Besides this, for most of the voter and in most constituencies, the main issues during that period were local, or at most regional. The really great issues confronting the nation, relating to the survival of India as a democratic state, economic development, national security, foreign policy, seemed hardly to figure at all. The political map of India was seemingly transformed, and the Congress for the first time seemed to be cracking up. This was not so much because of a nationwide revulsion against it; but because of more effective opposition tactics in which representatives of many different parties and groups, of many different ideological predilections and practical interests, participated. However, the voters did not give any clear indication of their alternate preferences, except in certain local and State situations.[96] The elections "have produced a mixed bag altogether. It is amply clear that the electorate does not want the Congress. It is not very clear what it does want."[97] The 1967 elections was thus beginning of emergence of regional and local parties, which later had influence on the national politics and elections.

However, with the passage of time, the concurrent nature of elections was lost due to dissolution of the elected bodies before the expiry of their maximum duration of five years. The cycle of simultaneous elections was broken up by the dissolution of several state assemblies in 1968 and 1969, the dissolution of the House of the People (4th Lok Sabha) in 1970, and the general elections that followed in 1971. The term of Fifth Lok Sabha was extended till 1977 due to declaration of emergency under Article 352. The Eighth, Tenth, Fourteenth, and Fifteenth Lok Sabha could complete their full five year terms; whereas the terms of the Sixth, Seventh, Ninth, Eleventh, Twelfth, and Thirteenth Lok Sabha were shortened due to premature dissolution. Similar problems regarding period of time were also faced by various State Assemblies. With the change in Indian political scenario, the regional political parties not only increased in number, but also registered their presence in the elections to the concerned State Assemblies.

In the present scenario, atleast one part of the country is witnessing an election throughout any given year. These premature dissolutions and extension interrupted the cycle of simultaneous elections. This resulted in burden in terms of time, energy and money on the voters, political parties and their leaders and the election authorities. Consequently, the country is continuously in an election mode. This highlights the need for simultaneous elections as against the fragmented and staggered election cycle prevalent currently.

9.6 Recommendations of Various Committees on Simultaneous Elections

(i) The Franchise Committee Report of 1932

The Franchise Committee Report of 1932[98], looking into franchise issues, suggested that the franchise for the Assembly should be the same as for the provincial councils as it involved the preparation of only one electoral roll.

"There is also the complication that it is the present practice to hold elections both for the provincial councils and for the Legislative Assembly on the same days. This arrangement has been devised partly to meet the convenience of voters who often have to travel considerable distances to the poll, and partly to avoid a double stoppage of ordinary administrative activity. It also suits candidates and political parties. But if there were to be adult franchise both for the provincial and for the federal legislatures, it would be necessary either to have a polling machinery which could deal at the same time with about 130 million electors, each entitled to cast votes for two different constituencies and candidates, or to duplicate the whole process at different times."[99]

The Franchise Committee Report of 1932, therefore, clearly provides a historical background for the concept of simultaneous elections and underlines the efficiency, convenience and coherence attainable through synchronized electoral cycles.

(ii) Election Commission of India First Annual Report in 1983

Election Commission in its first Annual Report in 1983[100], supported the notion of conducting concurrent elections for both the House of the People and the State Legislative Assemblies. Seven compelling reasons for holding simultaneous elections to the House of the People and State Legislative Assemblies were expounded which are as follows:

a) *Considerable savings on the colossal avoidable administrative and other expenditure incurred on account of holding of separate general elections, (Lok Sabha and State Legislative Assemblies).*

b) *Substantial economy through revision of electoral rolls for the House of the People and the State Legislative Assemblies simultaneously instead of undertaking them on a countrywide basis twice over in two different operations.*

c) *For the conduct of elections, civilian personnel running into about twenty-five lakh officers and staff and a few lakh police personnel are deployed every time for about two to three months, seriously affecting their normal duties.*

d) *During elections, whether for the Lok Sabha or the assemblies, the entire administrative set up throughout the country slows down considerably and all other normal functions and activities of the Government, including developmental work, are pushed to the background. These create a lot of hardships and sufferings to the common man. The situation continues for about two months during the conduct of every general election (Lok Sabha and State Legislative Assemblies).*

e) *Whereas changes in the administrative set up including transfers that become necessary in the normal course are not permitted under the broad guidelines issued by the Election Commission, there are considerable pressures prior to the issue of the notification calling for a general election to make wholesale changes, particularly at the district level.*

f) *On account of the de-linking of the general elections to the House of the People from that of the State Legislative Assemblies, there is a duplication of the expenditure incurred by the candidates contesting elections and political parties, which results in the pumping in of considerable resources that indirectly affects money supply in the economy. Further, by such delinking, the candidates for parliamentary elections need more money and resources to fight the election singlehanded over a wide area without the backing and co-operation of companion candidates of the assembly segments. This also, it is suspected, tends to lead to difficulties for candidates to keep within the ceiling for election expenses.*

(iii) National Commission to Review the Working of the Constitution (NCRWC) Report, 2002

The National Commission to Review the Working of the Constitution, headed by Shri Justice M.N. Venkatachalaiah in its Report, 2002[101] also recognized the need to restore simultaneous elections.

(iv) Parliamentary Standing Committee Report (2015)

The Standing Committee on Personnel, Public Grievances, Law and Justice under Chairmanship of Dr. E.M. Sudarsana Natchiappan made a systematic study of the matters involved in holding of elections in 2015. The Committee submitted its report on 'Feasibility of Holding Simultaneous Elections to House of People (Lok Sabha) and State Legislative Assemblies' on December 17, 2015. The committee emphasized on need for holding simultaneous elections. The Committee noted that the holding of simultaneous elections to Lok Sabha and state assemblies would reduce: (i) the massive expenditure that is currently incurred for the conduct of separate elections; (ii) the policy paralysis that results from the imposition of the Model Code of Conduct during election time; and (iii) impact on delivery of essential services and (iv) burden on crucial manpower that is deployed during election time.[102]

(v) Law Commission Reports recommending Simultaneous Elections

The Law Commission of India from time to time has deliberated on number of issues related to the conduct of elections. In its reports of 1999, 2015 and 2018 (draft), the Commission has recommended the adoption of the practice of simultaneous elections to reduce the encumbrances of asynchronous elections on citizens, political parties and government authorities.

(a) 170th Law Commission Report (1999)

The Law Commission under the Chairmanship of Justice B P Jeevan Reddy, submitted its 170th Report in May 1999. The Commission had stated:

> *"This cycle of elections every year, and in the out of season, should be put an end to. We must go back to the situation where the elections to Lok Sabha and all the Legislative Assemblies are held at once. It is true that we cannot conceive or provide for all the situations and eventualities that may arise whether on account of the use of article 356 (which of course has come down substantially after the decision of Supreme Court in S.R. Bommai v. Union of India) or for other reasons, yet the holding of a separate election to a Legislative Assembly should be an exception and not the rule. The rule ought to be 'one election once in five years for Lok Sabha and all the Legislative Assemblies' ".*[103]

(b) 180th Draft report of the Law Commission, 2018

The Law Commission of India under the Chairmanship of Justice B.S. Chauhan was called upon to study the issue regarding holding of simultaneous elections to the House of the People and the State Legislative Assemblies by Department of Legal Affairs. The Commission examined legal and constitutional questions related to the conduct of simultaneous elections. The 180th draft report of the Commission on "Simultaneous Elections" was released on August 30, 2018. Some of the significant recommendations made by the Commission in the draft report are as follows:[104]

- **The Commission observed that was simultaneous elections will be beneficial and will:** (i) save public funds; (ii) lessen the strain on the administrative setup and security forces; (iii) ensure the timely implementation of government policies; and (iv) make sure that the administrative machinery is working on development projects rather than campaigning.

- **Need for changes in constitutional and legal framework for conducting simultaneous elections:** The Commission stated that simultaneous elections are not permissible within the existing framework of the Constitution. Appropriate amendments to the Constitution, the Representation of the People Act of 1951, and the Rules of Procedure of the Lok Sabha and State Assemblies, will be needed to facilitate simultaneous elections to the Lok Sabha and State Legislative Assemblies Additionally, the Commission recommended that the constitutional amendments are required to be ratified by at least 50% of the states.

- **Framework for synchronisation of elections:** The Commission suggested three options to synchronise elections in India. These were:

- **Option 1-** The Commission suggested advancing or delaying some state elections so that the Lok Sabha and all state assemblies might have elections at the same time in 2019. It mentioned that, in addition to the Lok Sabha elections, five states—Andhra Pradesh, Arunachal Pradesh, Odisha, Sikkim, and Telangana—are scheduled to hold elections in 2019. It suggested the following adjustments be made to other state assemblies' election schedules:

- **Assembly elections scheduled before Lok Sabha elections:** Elections for four states—Mizoram, Rajasthan, Madhya Pradesh, and Chhattisgarh—are scheduled for late 2018 or early January 2019. By amending the Constitution, the duration of these legislatures may be increased to coincide with Lok Sabha elections.

- **Assembly elections scheduled immediately after Lok Sabha elections:** If there is political agreement, elections to four legislatures (Haryana, Jharkhand, Maharashtra, and Delhi) may be held in conjunction with Lok Sabha elections, if the states dissolve their assembly willingly beforehand, or by operation of law.

- **Assembly elections in remaining states:** Elections to the remaining 16 states and Puducherry might take place by the end of 2021. These assemblies will have term for 30 months, or till June 2024, whichever comes first. This will necessitate a constitutional amendment in order to either shorten or lengthen the terms of the several assemblies.

- Subsequently, elections to the Lok Sabha and state assemblies might then take place concurrently starting in 2024.
- **Option 2:** If assembly elections are held in 2019 and 2021, as previously mentioned, it will only be necessary to hold elections twice every five years.
- **Option 3:** If simultaneous elections are not possible, then the Commission suggested that all elections that are scheduled in a given calendar year be held concurrently. The timing of such election should be conducive to all state legislatures involved and the Lok Sabha (if dissolved earlier). The Constitution and the Representation of the People Act, 1951 both will need to be amended in order to implement this option.
- **No-confidence motion:** The Commission pointed out that if a resolution of no confidence is passed, the term of the state assembly or Lok Sabha may be curtailed. It suggested making the necessary changes to convert the "no-confidence motion" into a "constructive vote of no-confidence." In a constructive vote of no confidence, the current government may be overthrown only if there is confidence in a different government. It also suggested limiting the number of such motions during the term of the House or Assembly.
- **Hung House/ Assembly:** In case of hung House/ Assembly, where no party gets absolute majority to form the government, the Commission recommended that the President/ Governor should give a chance to the largest party along with their pre or post-poll coalition partners to form the government. If the government cannot still be formed, the impasse may be resolved by calling an all-party meeting. If this doesn't work, midterm elections might be held. The Commission suggested making the necessary amendments to ensure that any new Lok Sabha or Assembly established following midterm elections would only be constituted for the remaining period of the previous term, not the full five years.
- **Amendment to anti-defection laws:** The Commission suggested that suitable amendments be made to anti-defection laws to ensure

that all disqualification issues resulting from defection are decided by the presiding officer within six months.

(vi) Working paper by NITI Aayog, 2017

NITI Aayog Working paper on "Analysis of Simultaneous Elections: the What, Why and How" 2017 deliberated upon the proposal to conduct elections to the House of the People and the State Legislative Assembly, simultaneously analyzing the existing constitutional provisions, financial and logistical implications related to it. It indicated the desirability of holding simultaneous elections on more than one account.

(vi) Report of the six-member High-Level Committee under the Chairmanship of Shri Ram Nath Kovind, Former President, 2024

In September 2023, the Union Government constituted six-member High-Level Committee under the Chairmanship of Shri Ram Nath Kovind, Former President to "examine and make recommendations for holding simultaneous elections" in the Lok Sabha, state assemblies, and local bodies. The panel was assigned with the task of suggesting specific amendments to the Constitution and any other legal changes necessary to enable simultaneous elections and other related aspects. Major suggestions and recommendations made by the Committee are as follows: [105]

- The Committee has recommended that simultaneous election be held in the country. The committee has observed that a climate of uncertainty is created by regular elections. The simultaneous elections will provide stability and predictability in governance by reducing disruption and policy paralysis. Simultaneous election will boost turnout while cutting expenses. Also holding elections at the same time promotes better government spending, more investments, slower inflation, and faster economic growth.
- The Committee suggested a framework for concurrent elections, which necessitates for suitable amendments to the Constitution. All state assemblies and municipal bodies should be dissolved as a one-time action, regardless of the remaining term, at the time of the next Lok Sabha election. This will harmonize all elections. The Committee suggested simultaneously holding elections for the Lok Sabha, all State Assemblies, and local bodies within 100 days from then.

- The amendments should provide for designating an 'Appointed date' (being the day of the first meeting of the newly constituted House of the People) after which the conduct of elections to the State Legislative Assemblies (for the constitution of the State Legislative Assemblies) will take place. The tenure of all such Houses will expire with the tenure of the House of the People. For the constitution of the new Houses, the Election Commission of India will conduct simultaneous elections for the House of the People and the State Legislative Assemblies together. Where any State Legislative Assembly is dissolved on account of no-confidence motion, a hung House, or any other event, fresh elections will be held for such new House with its tenure ending with that of the House of the People.

- The Committee has recommended that for the purpose of making synchronised elections effective, a Constitution Amendment Bill shall be introduced in the Parliament amending Article 83 (Duration of Houses of Parliament) and Article 172 (Duration of State Legislatures) of the Constitution. This Constitution Amendment will not need ratification by the States. Another Constitution Amendment Bill will be introduced for insertion of Article 324A for elections to Municipalities and Panchayats, passed with ratification by the states.

- Thus the Committee observed that ratification by the states will not be required for constitutional amendments pertaining to the term of state assemblies and Parliament. However, constitutional amendments in relation to local bodies must be ratified by at least half of the states.

- The committee also suggested the way out in case there is a hung assembly. A legislature is elected for a five-year term. Therefore, if there is a hung legislature at any point of time, they would be out of sync for the following simultaneous election. The Committee suggested holding new elections for a hung legislature or local body with a reduced term in order to remedy this. For the simultaneous election, the shortened term will be equal to the remaining portion of the five-year cycle.

- The committee opined that there is need for Single electoral roll. Two constitutional authorities -Election Commission of India and State Election Commissions- supervise election process. Election Commission of India (ECI) for both Houses of Parliament, State Legislative Assemblies and Councils, President, and Vice-President; and State Election Commissions (SECs) for local entities. Preparation of electoral roll by SECs is administered by respective state laws. Some state laws permit SECs to prepare separate electoral rolls, while others allow them to use the electoral roll prepared by ECI.

- This will lessen redundancy and duplication across multiple agencies. The Committee suggested that ECI shall be the authority to create the unified electoral roll after consulting with SECs. An amendment to the Constitution will be needed to implement single electoral roll. The Committee also observed that the constitutional amendments in this regard are required to be ratified by atleast half of the states in order to become effective.

- The Committee recommended that ECI and SECs need to undertake planning and estimation for logistical arrangements around the time of the rollout.

9.7 Views Expressed on Simultaneous Elections

Former President, Shri Pranab Mukherjee, on a number of occasions has favoured simultaneous elections. While interacting with students on Teachers' Day in September 2016.

"With some election or the other throughout the year, normal activities of the government come to a standstill because of code of conduct,"

"This is an idea the political leadership should think of. If political parties collectively think, we can change it.... The Election Commission can also put in their idea and efforts on holding the polls together and that will be highly beneficial," he said[106]

Addressing a seminar on "Strategies for Empowering Young and Future Voters" the 7th National Voters' Day celebrations, Shri Pranab Mukherjee opined, *"There are talks of simultaneous elections in the political circles. It could be possible if the political parties seriously arrive at a consensus. It may be possible because it can remove a lot of inconvenience in terms of management,"* However, he added that the Election Commission should take the initiative.[107]

Again in his address to the nation on the eve of Republic Day in 2017[108], expressing his views on the desirability of holding simultaneous elections, he said,

"The time is also ripe for a constructive debate on electoral reforms and a return to the practice of the early decades after independence when elections to Lok Sabha and state assemblies were held simultaneously."

"It is for the Election Commission to take this exercise forward in consultation with political parties," he said.

Shri Nasim Zaidi, Former Chief Election Commissioner, speaking in the seminar on "Strategies for Empowering Young and Future Voters" on the eve of the 7th National Voters' Day celebrations had said, *"The commission, with certain additional resources, can undertake the exercise of simultaneous elections in future." But, he said, there are two pre-conditions. "One, there should be an amendment in the Constitution through a process of political consensus and we will need some additional resources in terms of electronic voting machines, etc."*[109]

Prime Minister Shri Narendra Modi, speaking at a conference of chief ministers and chief justices of high courts in April 2016, had supported the idea of simultaneous elections saying that otherwise, *"things get stalled and a lot of time is spent on elections".*[110]

However, not everyone is in the support of this idea. Shri Jagdeep Chhokar, founder-member of the Association for Democratic Reforms (ADR) has said:

"This is against democracy because trying to force an artificial cycle of elections and restricting the choice for voters, is not correct. Amending the Constitution for goods and services tax(GST) took 16 years, and for conducting simultaneous elections about six amendments to the Constitution are needed; this is not feasible considering the current political scenario of the country,"[111]

The government has also opened a discussion in 2016 through its MyGov platform on conducting simultaneous polls to Lok Sabha and state assemblies inviting comments on proposal by 15 October 2016.[112] There were on five indicative questions for the same which were as follows: [113]

- Is it desirable to hold simultaneous elections? What are the pros and cons?

- If simultaneous elections are held, then for the first time what happens to Assemblies whose scheduled tenure either ends before or after the proposed date of holding elections?
- Should the term of the Lok Sabha and Assemblies be fixed?
- What would happen in case by-elections are necessitated in between terms?
- What happens in case the ruling party or coalition loses majority in between term, either in the Lok Sabha or in Assemblies?

9.8 Need for Simultaneous Elections

(i) MCC Slows down the pace of Development

Frequent imposition of the Model Code of Conduct (MCC) causes policy paralysis and slows down the pace of the developmental programmes. The Model Code of conduct comes into operation from the date of announcement of election schedule by the Election Commission and remains operative till the process of elections is completed. During Lok Sabha elections, the code is applicable throughout the country and during elections to the Vidhan sabha, in the entire state. While the model code is in effect and applicable in the designated area, only routine governmental activities can be carried out and development initiatives, welfare schemes, capital projects, and other initiatives are essentially put on hold.

Though it is alleged that the MCC comes into play only from the date of announcement of elections; however, political parties in power start their preparation much before and come out with various populist measures to ensure their win in the elections.

During general elections in India, the Model Code of Conduct (MCC) is enforced across the country to ensure free and fair elections. In the most recent Lok Sabha elections 2024, the MCC remained in effect for 82 days.[114] During this period, several implications arise for the government. Primarily, governance-related activities and policy decisions are restricted, particularly those that could influence voter behaviour. Development projects, welfare schemes, and appointments are often paused, which can delay essential public services. Additionally, the government is barred from launching new schemes or making significant announcements, impacting both the pace and scope of governance during the election period. When considering separate elections for the Lok Sabha and state assemblies, the repeated enforcement of the Model Code of Conduct (MCC) at both national and state levels poses significant challenges to governance. Each time elections are held in different states, the MCC is enforced, leading to frequent pauses in governmental decision-making and project implementation. This disruption hinders the delivery of public goods and services, as governments are restricted from initiating new policies or continuing key development projects. The repetitive enforcement of the MCC not only affects governance efficiency but also slows down the overall progress of public welfare initiatives across states.

According to data from the Election Commission of India, the Model Code of Conduct (MCC) was in force for a total of 676 days between 2019 and 2024, covering both Lok Sabha and Vidhan Sabha elections. (Table 1) This implies that, on average, India spends approximately 113 days each year under the MCC. In a country with a population of 1.5 billion, the restriction of development and welfare activities for such a significant portion of the year raises serious concerns. This recurring pause in governance and policy implementation presents a challenge for ensuring consistent development and service delivery, thereby warranting further examination of its broader socio-economic implications.

Table 1

Enforcement of Model Code of Conduct Each Year in India											
2019		2020		2021		2022		2023		2024	
Jharkhand	50 days	Bihar	42 days	Assam	64 days	Goa	51 days	Meghalaya	43 days	Loksabha	82 days
Haryana	30 days	NCT of Delhi	30 days	Kerala		Manipur		Nagaland		Andhra Pradesh	
Maharashtra				Puducherry		Punjab		Tripura		Arunachal Pradesh	
Loksabha	71 days			Tamil Nadu		Uttarakhand		Chattisgarh	54 days	Odisha	
Andhra Pradesh				West Bengal		Uttar Pradesh		Madhya Pradesh		Sikkim	
Arunachal Pradesh						Gujarat	36 days	Mizoram		Jammu & Kashmir	52 days
Odisha						Himachal Pradesh	62 days	Rajasthan		Haryana	
Sikkim								Telangana			
Total	160 days	Total	72 days	Total	64 days	Total	149 days	Total	97 days	Total	154 days

Source: Election Commission of India

The Parliamentary Standing committee states:

> *"The imposition of Model Code of Conduct (MCC) puts on hold the entire development programme and activities of the Union and State Governments in*

the poll bound State. It even affects the normal governance. Frequent elections lead to imposition of MCC over prolonged periods of time. This often leads to policy paralysis and governance deficit".[115]

(ii) Cost Efficiency

The Election Commission is holding multiple elections every year. Conducting the elections in multiple phases results in a large amount of expenses for the country. In addition to the regular elections, a number of bye-elections are also conducted. This also places a significant strain on the government's finances. Frequent elections put extra financial strain on the government's exchequer. Each year, the Government of India and respective State Governments incur huge expenditure on organizing, managing, and overseeing elections. In addition to the government, political parties and candidates contesting elections also have to spend a lot of money and incur huge expenditures.

The candidates have to incur expenditure on various logistical needs to reaching out to the electorates. If the expenses of political parties are also added, the amount will increase further. While political parties spend money on running their electoral machinery during elections, arranging prominent leaders' campaigns, and other necessary activities; candidates typically incur expenses for traveling to their constituencies, general publicity, planning outreach events for voters, etc.

With regards to the expenditure incurred by candidates and political parties, the ECI vide Rule 90 of the Conduct of Election Rules, 1961 as amended on January 6, 2022 prescribes maximum limits for election expenditures by a candidate.[116] After the amendment, the present limit is Rs. 95 lakhs per candidate for a parliamentary constituency (i.e for elections to Lok Sabha) in larger states like UP, Bihar, Madhya Pradesh etc. This limit is Rs. 40 lakhs for an assembly constituency in the same States. However, there is no such limit prescribed for expenditure by political parties. In actual practice, the candidates and political parties spend significantly more than the prescribed expenditure limits in their attempt to win elections. The compulsion to spend more is consequently blamed as one of the factors for corruption and black-money in the country.

According to the data provided by the Election Commission, expenditure on elections relates to: setting up of the polling stations and making necessary arrangements therein; payment of TA/DA etc. to polling personnel /

counting staff; making transport arrangements for personnel involved in polling and counting duties; making infrastructure facilities at polling booths / counting centres; purchasing election material to be utilized for election; and other expenditures for smooth conduct of polling and counting.

Huge Expenditure incurred during Election is one of the major concern. Conducting elections on such a vast scale is an extremely difficult task for the Election Commission of India, requiring careful planning to safeguard the voting rights of the country's diverse electorate. The expenditure on organizing Lok Sabha elections has increased significantly over the years. For example, India's first general election in 1951-52, conducted over 68 phases, incurred a relatively modest expenditure of Rs 10.5 crore.[117] In contrast, the 2019 general election saw costs soar to Rs 50,000 crore ($7 billion), as reported by the Centre for Media Studies.[118] Based on these trends, the 2024 election is projected to nearly double this expenditure, potentially reaching Rs 1,00,000 crore.

Table 2

Total Expenditure by Parties during Assembly Elections, 2022

Mode of expenditure incurred	Total Expenditure incurred by political parties during Goa, Manipur, Punjab, Uttar Pradesh & Uttarakhand Assembly Elections, 2022 (in Rs Cr)						Total Expenditure
	Central Headquarters	State Units					
		Goa	Manipur	Punjab	Uttar Pradesh	Uttarakhand	
By Cash	0.1903	0.048	8.7260	0.152	0.1640	0.0017	**9.282**
By Cheque/DD	256.374	21.246	12.765	31.146	51.944	30.9726	**404.448**
Remaining unpaid	28.355	0.526	1.004	2.652	21.130	2.704	**56.371**
Total	**284.92**	**21.82**	**22.495**	**33.95**	**73.238**	**33.678**	**470.101**

Source- Association for Democratic Reforms

In a vast country like India, with approximately 968 million voters, elections are a frequent occurrence. The expenditures for state assembly (Vidhan Sabha) elections are distinct and separate from those incurred during the Lok Sabha elections. For instance, during the Assembly elections in Goa,

Manipur, Punjab, Uttar Pradesh, and Uttarakhand in 2022, the total expenditure amounted to Rs 470 crore, a figure solely reflecting the spending by political parties.[119] (Table 2) The expenditure by the states themselves on these elections is significantly higher, further adding to the financial burden of the electoral process in India.(Table 3)

Table 3

Party wise expenditure during Assembly Elections, 2022

Political Party	Total Expenditure incurred by political parties during Goa, Manipur, Punjab, Uttar Pradesh & Uttarakhand Assembly Elections, 2022 (in Rs Cr)						Total Expenditure (in Rs Cr)
	Central Headquarters	State Units					
		Goa	Manipur	Punjab	Uttar Pradesh	Uttarakhand	
BJP	86.374	13.986	11.402	18.063	66.784	26.539	**223.148**
INC	72.536	7.554	10.471	0.033	4.964	7.092	**102.65**
BSP	68.646	-	-	0	0	0	**68.646**
AITC	40.778	0	-	-	-	-	**40.778**
SAD	0	-	-	15.72	-	-	**15.72**
AAP	8.730	0.0344	-	0.0983	0.2778	0.026	**9.167**
NCP	5.28	0	0.054	-	-	-	**5.334**
RLD	1.6493	-	-	-	0.0135	0	**1.663**
AIMIM	0.0175				1.172	0	**1.189**
Shivsena	0.573	0.2458	0.0439	-	0	-	**0.863**
NPF	0	-	0.45	-	-	-	**0.45**
CPI	0.272	-	0.074	0.025	0.0072	0.0213	**0.40**
CPI(ML)(L)	0.064	-	-	0.011	0.019	0	**0.094**
Grand Total	**284.92**	**21.82**	**22.495**	**33.95**	**73.238**	**33.678**	**470.101**

(-) Did not contest in the State Assembly election

Source- Association for Democratic Reforms

Advocates of the 'One Nation, One Election' proposal argue that the separate expenditures on state assembly elections could be significantly reduced through simultaneous elections. They assert that political parties allocate approximately 35% of their budgets to campaigns and publicity, a cost that could be minimized if both Lok Sabha and assembly elections were held together.[120] This synchronization would eliminate the need for duplicating efforts in campaign management, voter outreach, and publicity at different times, thereby streamlining the electoral process and reducing overall expenditure for political parties and the state.

(iii) Causes hardship to citizens

Frequent elections cause disruption to normal life of citizens and effects the functioning of essential services. People face inconvenience due to disruption of road traffic and noise pollution due to holding of political rallies. Simultaneous elections can limit these disturbances to a certain pre-determined period of time. Frequent elections also result in uncertainty and instability, upsetting supply chains, business investments and economic growth.

(iv) Reduced Disruption to Governance

With continuing cycle of elections in one or the other part of the country, the political parties, including the ruling party at the Centre and the State(s), tend to invest their time and energy more on the elections, rather than on the governance, deviating attention from core issues of good governance and development, to campaigning for elections. Restricting the elections to once in a five years' affair will help in dedicating time and resources towards development activities.

(v) Administrative efficiency

Regular deployment of government officials and security forces for elections hinders discharge of their duties. The crucial manpower which is often deployed for prolonged periods on election duties disrupts government machinery. The polling booths are mostly located in schools, whether Government or private. Engaging school staff and teaching personnel for election duties, compromises their primary duty of imparting education as schools remain closed even prior to elections. Similar is the situation with the employees of Central and State Governments and the PSUs who are assigned election duty.

The security forces are deployed normally throughout the elections and they remain mobile from one place to another. As one or the other state goes for elections every six months, the situation leads to security forces remaining locked in for prolonged period of time, taking away a big portion of such armed and police forces, which could otherwise be better deployed for other internal security purposes, which is their core function.

(vi) Increased Voter turnout

Further a number of studies have indicated that combining national and state elections could potentially increase voter-participation-a hallmark of representative democracy. Staggered elections induce 'voters' fatigue' and present a significant challenge in ensuring their participation. In simultaneous elections, citizens could vote for national and state elections simultaneously which could reduce voters' fatigue.

9.9 Challenges for 'One Nation, One Election'

Opponents of the idea say that simultaneous elections will compromise the federal nature of governance, weaken democratic diversity, and introduce administrative complexities that will far outweigh the benefits. They are of the opinion that neither the cost of elections nor the restrictions of the model code of conduct are determining concerns for holding concurrent elections. Elections every five years are undoubtedly less expensive than multiple elections held at various intervals; however with simultaneous elections the money saved will be less than Rs 5,000 crore annually. Should that be the deciding factor for an economy like India?[121] Further they are of the opinion that the restrictions of the model code of conduct will only apply for a limited period and its application is nationwide only when there's a national election. It's a minor concern at the state level. According to them, elections which are the most significant manifestation of democracy, shouldn't be judged based on their cost or by the conduct required for their fair implementation. The term of 17 state assemblies will be shortened to hold synchronized elections in 2029; this violates the basic structure of the Constitution. For violating the basic structure of the Constitution, the expenditure and consequential savings for conducting synchronized elections is being given as a justification.[122]

Arguing against 'One Nation, One Election' they opine that it contradicts the character of our country. When we do not have one religion, one language, one culture then why one elections. We're a union of states and the differences and diversity constitute our wealth which make us special and significant. Secondly, it also likely to lead to prioritizing national issues over local ones. They also suspect that it has a tendency to convert a federal structure into a unitary structure, over time and the regional concerns of smaller states will be masked by the national issues and demands of the Centre. Doubts are also being raised that 'One Nation, One Election' will exacerbate the trend of parliamentary elections becoming increasingly presidential and push our multi-party system towards a one-party state. Instead of expanding and deepening our democracy, it will narrow our democracy by straightjacketing the opportunity to vote. The concerns raised regarding synchronized elections are elaborated below:

(i) Logistical Issues

While proponents of the 'One Nation, One Election' proposal argue that simultaneous elections would reduce the overall expenditure, there are concerns that certain costs may, in fact, increase. A NITI Aayog paper supporting this proposal found that the central government would need to invest over Rs 9,300 crore to procure additional Electronic Voting Machines (EVMs) and Voter Verifiable Paper Audit Trail (VVPAT) systems.[123] Moreover, the requirement for extra security personnel and election officials to manage the larger-scale simultaneous elections could further escalate operational costs, raising questions about the financial feasibility of the initiative in its entirety.

The elections to the House of the People and State Assemblies are held using EVMs. Presently, same EVMs are used for elections in various States. Therefore, conducting simultaneous elections necessitates procurement of more EVMs and also entails the problem regarding their storage. Due to the paucity of warehousing facilities, many states and UTs are compelled to store the EVMs in private buildings and educational institutions. There will be an increased demand for safe, practical storage facilities with increased number of EVMs. Increased number of EVMs will require more polling material, polling staff and additional vehicles. Ensuring smooth, peaceful and impartial polls also needs services of a significant number of polling officials from government organisations for significantly prolonged periods.

(ii) Constitutional and Legal Changes

Holding concurrent elections would require a series of amendments to the Constitution, in provisions governing timing of elections, tenure of legislatures, and electoral procedures. These constitutional amendments would requires approval by a two-thirds majority in both houses of Parliament, as well as ratification by at least half of India's states. Modifications would also be required in the laws relating to elections like the Representation of the People Act, 1951, to align election schedules.

(iii) Overlook the diverse issues and aspirations of individual states

One Nation One Election could undermine the unique political dynamics and regional interests of different states in India, as it promotes a uniform election cycle. It might lead to neglect of various issues and aspirations of the states, resulting in a disregard for their specific requirements. Different states in India have different political ideologies, priorities, and policy preferences. Having synchronised elections would undermine the unique political dynamics and regional interests of different states. One Nation, One Election may lead to disruption in policy continuity, as changes in national-level governments may lead to significant shifts in state level governance, which could potentially impact long-term planning and development.

(iv) Potential Impact on Local Issues

Critics argue that with simultaneous elections national issues will dominate the discourse which may overshadow state-level concerns. The focus on state-specific challenges will be reduced leading to disconnect between voters' expectations and the outcomes of state elections. Opponents have also raised concerns regarding centralisation of power, giving the ruling party at the national level greater power over state politics.

(v) Contradicts India's Diversity and Federal Structure

Opposition parties such as the Congress, the Left, and the Trinamool Congress have voiced their disapproval, arguing that 'One Nation, one Election' proposal weakens India's federal structure and could diminish the autonomy of state governments. It will give the central government an upper hand in state matters by centralizing power and decision-making, potentially reducing the autonomy of states and their ability to address local issues effectively.

(vi) Need for significant financial resources

Significant financial resources are needed for campaigning during simultaneous elections. Smaller parties or candidates with limited funding may struggle to compete on a larger scale, potentially creating an imbalance in political representation and limiting the diversity of voices in the democratic process.

(vii) Logistical and Security Challenges

Implementing synchronized elections across a vast and diverse country like India poses significant logistical & security challenges like ensuring adequate security, efficient administration, and coördination among multiple stakeholders can be complex and may increase the risk of logistical failures or delays in conducting elections.

Before implementing 'One Nation, One Election' rule, the government and Election Commission of India needs to build consensus which can be achieved through transparent dialogue, consultations, and deliberations among various stakeholders that include political parties, civil society and citizens. Besides its benefits, there are issues which need to be adequately addressed before implementation which include:

- desirability to hold simultaneous elections,
- the pros and cons of synchronised elections,
- changes required in the constitutional and legal framework,
- practical preparations and investment needed in electoral infrastructure and technology,
- raising voter awareness about the advantages and challenges of simultaneous elections,
- potential impact on country's democratic processes.

The decision on its implementation should be a collective one, taking into account the intricacies involved and the variety of viewpoints being set forth. 'One Nation, One Election' policy should be well thought out, taking into account any potential effects on the democratic processes of the nation.

10. Conclusion

For Viksit Bharat governance based on the principles of democracy is paramount. Democracy can function only upon the faith of the people, which is built and regularly assessed through periodical elections to ascertain the popular will. In view of both long- and short term implications of the elections and manifestations for the future of democracy, there is a need to take a closer look at the process of administering elections in India and at the totality of the election process in a holistic manner. There are problems in the functioning of our electoral system that need to be rectified.

Frequent asynchronized elections causing disruption of the governance machinery, causing policy paralysis, and slowing down the pace of the developmental programmes is an area of concern. The government has approved the proposal to conduct synchronised elections across the country, aligning elections for the Lok Sabha, state assemblies, and local bodies under the "One Nation, One Election" plan. This, no doubt, will have significant benefits in terms of reducing costs, improving governance, and minimizing administrative disruption. However, to implement simultaneous elections, a delicate balance needs to be maintained between constitutional amendments, logistical preparedness, and preserving the federal spirit. To capitalize on the latent advantages of "One Nation, One Election," the government needs to follow a consultative approach to address concerns associated with it to build a consensus approach.

A constitution has to be a 'living document' that is capable of adapting to changing needs and requirements of people and society. It has to be dynamic, effective, and efficient, responding to the changing situations and growing needs of the citizens and meeting their expectations. However, at the same time, the intrinsic values and basic features of the Constitution, such as democracy, free and fair elections, and federalism, cannot be compromised. In this background, we need to examine and implement the 'one nation, one election' rule; introducing reforms in the domain of the electoral system without damaging the intrinsic character and framework of the Constitution. No doubt it is not an easy task; there will always be people who will view the changes with doubt and oppose them, and want the status quo to be continued throughout.

11. References

1. Philip Pettit, (2000), Democracy, Electoral and Contestatory, *Nomos* , 2000, Vol. 42, *Designing Democratic Institutions* pp. 105-144 at p. 106 Published by: American Society for Political and Legal Philosophy, https://www.jstor.org/stable/pdf/24219915.pdf?refreqid=fastly-default%3A9da92ee67ab678149c193d9745569815&ab_segments=0%2Fbasic

search_gsv2%2Fcontrol&origin=&initiator=&acceptTC=1 accessed on August 9, 2024

2. As held by the Supreme Court in a landmark case of *Kesavananda Bharati v. State of Kerala*, AIR 1973 SC 1461
3. *Mohinder Singh Gill & Anr vs The Chief Election Commissioner*, AIR 1978 SC 851
4. Quoted by Krishna Iyer, J. in Mohinder Singh Gill & Anr vs The Chief Election Commissioner, AIR 1978 SC 851
5. AIR 1978 SC 851
6. *Webster's dictionary, https://webstersdictionary1828.com/Dictionary/election*
7. *Black's Law Dictionary, 2nd Ed.,* https://thelawdictionary.org/election/ *accessed on Sept 3, 2024*
8. The Representation of the People Act, 1951, Section 2(d)
9. James S. Robbins, (1997), Introduction: Democracy and Elections, *The Fletcher Forum of World Affairs*, Vol. 21, No. 1 (Winter/Spring 1997), pp. 1- 13, at p. 1 The Fletcher School of Law and Diplomacy, https://www.jstor.org/stable/45288975 Accessed: 11-08-2024 02:58
10. Cees Van der Eijk, Mark N. Franklin, *Elections and Voters*, Palgrave Macmillan, 2009, page 1 https://ereader.perlego.com/1/book/2996245/16 accessed on Aug.31, 2024
11. *Id* at page 5
12. Wilson, W. [1885], *Congressional Government*, Boston: Houghton Mifflin
13. Bagehot, W. (1873), *The English Constitution*, Boston: Little Brown
14. D.E. Stokes, 'Voting', *International Encyclopedia of Social Sciences*, Vol. 16, New York, Free Press and Macmillan, 1968, p. 390.
15. J.W. Garner, *Political Science and Government, Calcutta*, World Press, 1951 (original American edition), 1935, p. 495.
16. D.E. Stokes, op.cit.
17. N.R. Inamdar, Theoretical Approaches to Elections: Implications for Outcomes of Elections Administration in India, *Indian Journal of Public Administration-Administering Elections in India* Vol. XXXVII, No. 3, July-Sept. 1991, pp. 267-281 at p. 269
18. John Stuart Mill, (1861), *Representative Government*, p.116, Batoche Books Kitchener 2001, https://socialsciences.mcmaster.ca/econ/ugcm/3ll3/mill/repgovt.pdf accessed on August 10, 2024
19. *Report of the Indian Round Table Conference Sub-Committees*, Vol. VI, pp.5, 30-31
20. *Constitution of India*, Article 326
21. *Constitution of India*, Article 325
22. *Constitution of India*, Articles 330 and 331
23. *Constitution of India*, Article 324.
24. *Constitution of India*, Article 54
25. Explanation to Article 54 added vide the Constitution (Seventieth Amendment) Act, 1992]

26. *Constitution of India*, Article 55 (1)
27. *Constitution of India*, Article 55(2)(a) &(b)
28. *Constitution of India*, Article 55(2)(c)
29. *Constitution of India*, Article 57
30. *Constitution of India*, Article 58 (1)
31. *Constitution of India*, Article 58 (2)
32. *Constitution of India*, Article 66 (1) &(2)
33. *Constitution of India*, Article 66 (3)
34. *Constitution of India*, Article 66 (4)
35. *Constitution of India*, Article 68
36. *Constitution of India*, Article 67
37. *Constitution of India*, Article 83 (2)
38. *Constitution of India*, AIR 1994 SC 1918
39. *Constitution of India*, Article 81 (2)(a)
40. *Constitution of India*, Article 81 (2)(b)
41. *Constitution of India*, Article 81 (3)
42. *Constitution of India*, Article 83(1)
43. *Constitution of India*, Article 172 (1)
44. *Constitution of India*, Article 172 (2)
45. *Constitution of India*, Article 326
46. S. S. Singh & Suresh Misra, Power of Election Commission: A Legal Perspective, *Indian Journal of Public Administration-Administering Elections in India* Vol. XXXVII, No. 3, July-Sept. 1991, pp.361-372
47. *Constitution of India*, Article 324 (1)
48. *Constitution of India*, Article 324 (2)
49. *Constitution of India*, Article 324 (3), (4) &(5)
50. *Constitution of India*, Article 324 (6)
51. *Constitution of India*, Article 330(1)
52. *Constitution of India*, Article 330(2)
53. *Constitution of India*, Article 331
54. *Constitution of India*, Article 332
55. *Constitution of India*, Article 333
56. *Constitution of India*, Article 334
57. *Constitution of India*, Article 243 (d)
58. *Constitution of India*, Article 243B (1)
59. *Constitution of India*, Article 243B(2)
60. *Constitution of India*, Article 243 (b)
61. *Constitution of India*, Article 243A
62. *Id* Clause 1
63. *Id* Clause 2&3
64. *Constitution of India*, Article 243E (1)
65. *Id* Clause 3& 4

66. *Constitution of India*, Article 243T (1)
67. *Id* Clause 2
68. *Id* Clause 3
69. *Id* Clause 4
70. *Constitution of India*, Article 243U
71. Sugato Dasgupta, et.al., Coordinated voting in sequential and simultaneous elections: someexperimental evidence, *Experimental Economics* 11 (2007), pp. 315 – 335.
72. Matthew Soberg Shugart, The Electoral Cycle and Institutional Sources of Divided Presidential Government, *The American Political Science Review* 89 (Juni 1995), pp. 327 – 343.
73. Satrio Alif Febriyanto, Fitra Arsil, and Qurrata Ayuni; Models of Simultaneous Elections around the World: The Influence of Government Systems on Election Implementation Methods, 175-186 at p. 177 in W. Waluyo et al. (eds.), *Proceedings of the International Conference for Democracy and National Resilience* (ICDNR 2023), Advances in Social Science, Education and Humanities Research 795, https://doi.org/10.2991/978-2-38476-148-7_16
74. Arjan H. Schakel dan Régis Dandoy, Electoral Cycles and Turnout in Multilevel Electoral Systems, *West European Politics* (2014), pp. 605 – 623.
75. Arjan H. Schakel dan Régis Dandoy, "Electoral Cycles and Turnout in Multilevel Electoral Systems," *West European Politics* (2014), pp. 605 – 623; Syamsuddin Haris, et.al., Position Paper: *Pemilu Nasional Serentak* 2019. Jakarta: Electoral Research Institute Lembaga Ilmu Pengetahuan Indonesia (2014).
76. South African Government, Elections, https://www.gov.za/about-sa/elections accessed on September5, 2024
77. Law Commission of India, *Draft Report- Simultaneous Elections*, 30 August 2018 Government of India
78. Cabinet accepts recommendations of High-Level Committee on Simultaneous Elections, 18 Sep, 2024, https://www.pmindia.gov.in/en/news_updates/cabinet-accepts-recommendations-of-high-level-committee-on-simultaneous-elections/?comment=disable accessed on Sept 20, 2024; PIB Delhi, Cabinet accepts recommendations of High-Level Committee on Simultaneous Elections, 18 Sept 2024; https://pib.gov.in/PressReleasePage.aspx?PRID=2056059, accessed on Sept 20, 2024
79. Preetha Nair, Government plans 3 Bills to implement 'One Nation One Poll', *The New Indian Express*, 30 Sep 2024 https://www.newindianexpress.com/nation/2024/Sep/30/government-plans-3-bills-to-implement-one-nation-one-poll
80. Bibek Debroy and Kishore Desai, "Analysis of simultaneous elections: The "What", "Why" And "How" available at:

https://legalaffairs.gov.in/sites/default/files/simultaneous_elections/NITI_AYOG_REPORT_2017.pdf, Law Commission of India, Draft Report-Simultaneous Elections, 30 August 2018
https://legalaffairs.gov.in/sites/default/files/simultaneous_elections/LCI_2018_DRAFT_REPORT.pdf

81. National Panchayati Raj Day, https://vikaspedia.in/social-welfare/rural-poverty-alleviation-1/national-panchayati-raj-day#:~:text=Your%20browser%20does%20not%20support%20the%20audio%20element.&text=The%20Constitution%20of%20India%20recognizes,local%20bodies%20(RLBs)/%20panchayats.
82. *Report on the Second General elections in India, 1957* -Volume I, General, Election Commission of India.
83. *Id* at 123, 124.
84. Richard Leonard Park, (1952), India's General Elections, *Far Eastern Survey* , Vol. 21, No. 1 (Jan. 9, 1952), pp. 1-8, published by Institute of Pacific Relations Stable https://www.jstor.org/stable/3024683, accessed on 08 Aug 2024
85. Broadcast speech of Prime Minister Nehru, November 22, 1951 quoted in Richard Leonard Park, (1952), India's General Elections, *Far Eastern Survey* , Vol. 21, No. 1 (Jan. 9, 1952), pp. 1-8, published by Institute of Pacific Relations Stable https://www.jstor.org/stable/3024683, accessed on 08 Aug 2024
86. The Representation of the People Act, 1950, Section 19. (The qualifying periods were added to the statutory provision by Order.)
87. Election Commission, *The Report on the First General Elections in India* 1951-52, Vol. I (General), Government of India, New Delhi, 1955.
88. Richard Leonard Park, (1952), India's General Elections, *Far Eastern Survey* , Vol. 21, No. 1 (Jan. 9, 1952), pp. 1-8, at p. 8 published by Institute of Pacific Relations Stable https://www.jstor.org/stable/3024683, accessed on 08 Aug 2024
89. James R. Roach, (1957), India's 1957 Elections, *Far Eastern Survey*, Vol. 26, No. 5 (May, 1957), pp. 65-78, Institute of Pacific Relations, https://www.jstor.org/stable/3024537 accessed on Oct 1, 2024
90. Myron Weiner, (1962), India's Third General Elections, *Asian Survey* , Vol. 2, No. 3 (May, 1962), pp. 3-18, University of California Press, https://www.jstor.org/stable/3023512 accessed on Oct 1, 2024
91. Samuel J. Eldersveld, The 1967 Indian Election: Patterns of Party Regularity and Defection, *Asian Survey*, Vol. 10, No. 11, Elections and Party Politics in India: A Symposium (Nov., 1970), pp. 1015-1030, Published by University of California Press
https://www.jstor.org/stable/2642821, Accessed on 04-10-2024
92. Norman D. Palmer, India's Fourth General Election, *Asian Survey*, Vol. 7, No. 5 (May, 1967), pp. 275-291, University of California Press,
https://www.jstor.org/stable/2642657
Accessed on 04-10-2024

93. Norman D. Palmer, India's Fourth General Election, *Asian Survey*, Vol. 7, No. 5 (May, 1967), pp. 275-291, University of California Press, https://www.jstor.org/stable/2642657
    94. Accessed on 04-10-2024
95. "The Numbers Game" (Delhi Letter from "A Political Correspondent"), *NOW*, Jan. 20, 1967, p. 9
96. Eric da Costa, The General Elections-XV; "Prospects of Nonviolent Revolution Disestablishing the Establishment," *The Economic Times*, Jan 30, 1967.
97. Norman D. Palmer, India's Fourth General Election, *Asian Survey*, Vol. 7, No.5 (May, 1967), pp. 275-291, at p. 289 University of California Press, https://www.jstor.org/stable/2642657 Accessed on 04-10-2024
98. Id at p. 290
99. *Sunday Standard*, March 12, 1967.
100. *Report of the Indian Franchise Committee, Volume I (*Calcutta: Government of India, Central Publication Branch, 1932), https://www.nottingham.ac.uk/research/groups/conferencing-the-international/documents/official-documents/travelling-committee-reports/report-of-the-indian-franchise-committee.pdf
101. *Report of the Indian Franchise Committee, Volume I (*Calcutta: Government of India, Central Publication Branch, 1932), https://www.nottingham.ac.uk/research/groups/conferencing-the-international/documents/official-documents/travelling-committee-reports/report-of-the-indian-franchise-committee.pdf
102. *Id* at para 17 at p. 17
103. Election Commission of India, First Annual Report (April, 1984).
104. https://legalaffairs.gov.in/national-commission-review-working-constitution-ncrwc-report
105. Prianka Rao, Standing Committee Report Summary Feasibility of holding simultaneous elections to Lok Sabha and State Legislative Assemblies, January 4, 2016, PRS Legislative Research https://prsindia.org/files/policy/policy_committee_reports/1451885664_SCR%20Summary-%20feasibility%20of%20holding%20simultaneous%20central%20and%20state%20elections_0.pdf

106. Law Commission of India (1999), *170th Report -Reform of the Electoral Laws,* para 7.2.1.1 p. 80 https://lawcommissionofindia.nic.in/cat_electoral_reforms/ accessed on Sept 1, 2024
107. PRS, Draft Report on Simultaneous Elections, https://prsindia.org/policy/report-summaries/draft-report-simultaneous-elections
108. PRS, Simultaneous Elections in India, https://prsindia.org/policy/report-summaries/simultaneous-elections-in-india
109. Komal Gupta, Government seeks public comments on simultaneous polls, 8 Sep 2016, https://www.livemint.com/Politics/uFkHsKsNfhHS14zBABu8WM/Government-seeks-public-comments-on-simultaneous-polls.html accessed on Oct 2, 2024
110. Pranab backs simultaneous polls New Delhi, Jan 26, 2017, DHNS, file:///C:/Users/dr%20sapna/Downloads/PRANAB%20BACKS%20SIMULTANEOUS%20POLLS%20(1).pdf accessed on Oct. 2, 2024
111. Press Trust of India, In his Republic Day speech, President bats for simultaneous polls, Business Standard, Jan 25 2017 https://www.business-standard.com/article/current-affairs/in-his-republic-day-speech-president-bats-for-simultaneous-polls-117012501067_1.html accessed on October 2, 2024
112. Pranab backs simultaneous polls New Delhi, Jan 26, 2017, DHNS, file:///C:/Users/dr%20sapna/Downloads/PRANAB%20BACKS%20SIMULTANEOUS%20POLLS%20(1).pdf accessed on Oct. 2, 2024
113. Komal Gupta, Government seeks public comments on simultaneous polls, 8 Sep 2016, https://www.livemint.com/Politics/uFkHsKsNfhHS14zBABu8WM/Government-seeks-public-comments-on-simultaneous-polls.html accessed on Oct 2, 2024
114. *Ibid*
115. *Ibid*
116. B. Phani Kumar &Bela Routh, Reference Note No. 45/RN/Ref/Nov/2016 -Simultaneous Elections to Lok Sabha, and State Legislative Assemblies, Members' Reference Service LARRDIS, Lok Sabha Secretariat, New Delhi, Nov. 2016 https://loksabhadocs.nic.in/Refinput/New_Reference_Notes/English/Simultaneous_election_to_Lok_Sabha_and_State_Legislative_Assemblies.pdf
117. taneous_election_to_Lok_Sabha_and_State_Legislative_Assemblies.pdf
118. News Article AL Jazeera Just how big is India's 2024 election? Find out in seven numbers, https://www.aljazeera.com/news/2024/3/16/india-announces-election-2024-seven-numbers-to-unpack-worlds-biggest-vote

119. The Parliamentary Standing committee, *79th Report. Feasibility of Holding Simultaneous Elections to the House of People (Lok Sabha) and State Legislative Assemblies*, 17 December, 2015, para 6.3 page 4, https://legalaffairs.gov.in/sites/default/files/simultaneous_elections/79th_Report.pdf
120. Election Commission of India, Press Note- Limits of candidate's expenses Enhanced, Jan 06, 2022, https://ceodelhi.gov.in/PDFFolder/ECI/PN-2_06012022%20(1).pdf
121. Lok Sabha election 2024: How much does it cost to hold elections in India? https://www.business-standard.com/elections/lok-sabha-election/lok-sabha-election-2024-how-much-does-it-cost-to-hold-elections-in-india-124041900352_1.html
122. Poll Expenditure, The 2019 Elections https://cmsindia.org/sites/default/files/2019-05/Poll-Expenditure-the-2019-elections-cms-report.pdf
123. Association for Democratic Reforms report, Analysis of Funds Collected and Expenditure Incurred by Political Parties during Goa, Manipur, Punjab, Uttar Pradesh & Uttarakhand Assembly Elections, 2022, https://adrindia.org/sites/default/files/Analysis_of_Funds_Collected_and_Expenditure_Incurred_by_Political_Parties_during_Goa_Manipur_Punjab_Uttar%20_Pradesh_%26_Uttarakhand_Assembly_Elections%2C_2022_English.pdf
124. The Economic Times, Record-breaking election spending set to ignite rural demand, feel experts Read more at: https://economictimes.indiatimes.com/news/elections/lok-sabha/india/record-breaking-election-spending-set-to-ignite-rural-demand-feel-experts/articleshow/109852310.cms?utm_source=contentofinterest&utm_medium=text&utm_campaign=cppst
125. Karan Thapar, One Nation, One Election: Does it restrict democracy?, *Indian Express*, Sept 30, 2024 accessed on Oct 1, 2024 https://indianexpress.com/article/opinion/columns/one-nation-one-election-restrict-democracy-9596050/
126. Kapil Sibal, One Nation, One Election: Yet another Jumla, 30 Sep 2024, https://www.newindianexpress.com/opinions/2024/Sep/29/one-nation-one-election-yet-another-jumla accessed on Oct. 1, 2024
127. R., Ananthakrishnan, G., Chandrasekaran, B., R, M., Staff, I., Arjunan, S., & K. (2018, July 14). Who said simultaneous posts cut expenditure? What about EVM costs? - Inmathi. Inmathi. https://inmathi.com/2018/07/14/who-said-simultaneous-posts-cut-expenditure-what-about-evmcosts/7683/

12. Bibliography

1. Agarala Easwara Reddi and D. Sundar Ram, Administering Clean and Fair Elections in India, *The Indian Journal of Public Administration,* Vol. XXXVII July-September, 1991 No.3, PP 310-323
2. Ahmad, Imtiaz. "Election studies in India." *Economic and Political Weekly* (1977): 1677-1680.
3. Ahuja, M. L. *Electoral politics and general elections in India, 1952-1998.* Mittal Publications, 1998.
4. Ahuja, M. L. *General Elections in India: Electoral Politics, Electoral Reforms, and Political Parties.* Icon Publishers, 2005.
5. Ahuja, M. L. *Handbook of General Elections and Electoral Reforms in India, 1952-1999.* Mittal Publications, 2000.
6. Amalia, Luky Sandra, et al. "Simultaneous elections and the rise of female representation in Indonesia." *Journal of Current Southeast Asian Affairs* 40.1 (2021): 50-72.
7. Anas, Hanif, Ratna Herawati, and Fifiana Wisnaeni. "Examining the Redesign of the National and Local Simultaneous General Elections." *Proceedings of the 1st International Workshop on Law, Economics and Governance, IWLEG 2022, 27 July 2022, Semarang, Indonesia.* 2023.
8. Annisa, Neng Nur. "Analysis of the Advantages and Disadvantages of Simultaneous Elections: Impacts on Indonesian Society and Technical Considerations in Their Implementation." *Khazanah Sosial* 2.3 (2020): 217-223.
9. Ar, Muhammad Misbahudholam, Rofik Rofik, and Ahmad Hanafi. "Expensive Political Costs in the 2024 Simultaneous Elections." *Jurnal Hukum dan Sosial Politik* 1.1 (2023): 01-20.
10. Aragonès, Enriqueta. *Simultaneous Elections.* BSE, Barcelona School of Economics, 2023.
11. AS, Yashwanth. "Simultaneous Elections in India." *Issue 3 Int'l JL Mgmt. & Human.* 3 (2020): 1862.
12. Bairagi, Ashutosh. "One Nation One Election in India: A Contemporary Need vis-a-vis a Matter of Mere Discussion." *Issue 2 Int'l JL Mgmt. & Human.* 5 (2022): 1726.
13. Bal, Mr Hartosh Singh. *"One Nation One Election: Simultaneous Elections.* Diss. OP Jindal Global University, 2018.
14. Banerjee, Mukulika. *Why India Votes?.* Routledge India, 2017.
15. Bansal, Meenakshi. "The Concept of One Nation One Election: An Analysis from Indian Perspective." *Think India Journal* 22.4 (2019): 3077-3084.

16. Bhagat, Parindu, and Mrs Purvi Pokharyal. "Conceptual Reforms One Nation–One Election" *Ilkogretim Online* 19.4 (2020): 3929-3935.
17. C.P. Bhambhri, Election and Political Change, *The Indian Journal of Public Administration*, Vol. XXXVII July-September, 1991 No.3, PP 302-306
18. Chakravarty, Praveen. One Nation, One Election: Why this kolaveri?, Deccan Herald, 29 September 2024, https://www.deccanherald.com/opinion/one-nation-one-election-why-this-kolaveri-3211523 accessed on Oct 1, 2024
19. Dasgupta, Sugato, et al. "Coordinated voting in sequential and simultaneous elections: some experimental evidence." *Experimental Economics* 11 (2008): 315-335.
20. Debroy, Bibek, and Kishore Desai. "Analysis of Simultaneous Elections: The 'What','Why'and 'How'." *Why," and" How* (2017).
21. Dehdari, Sirus H., Jaakko Meriläinen, and Sven Oskarsson. "Selective abstention in simultaneous elections: Understanding the turnout gap." *Electoral Studies* 71 (2021): 102302.
22. Election Commission and Electoral Reform, *The Indian Journal of Public Administration*, Vol. XXXVII July-September, 1991 No.3, PP 557-566
23. Electoral Reforms Suggested by Election Commission in Second Annual Report 1984, *The Indian Journal of Public Administration*, Vol. XXXVII July-September, 1991 No.3, PP 567-578
24. Electoral Reforms Suggested in the First Election Commission Report 1951, *The Indian Journal of Public Administration*, Vol. XXXVII July-September, 1991 No.3, PP 513-521
25. Electoral Reforms: Innovations and Improvements, *The Indian Journal of Public Administration*, Vol. XXXVII July-September, 1991 No.3, PP 534-556
26. Febriyanto, Satrio Alif, Fitra Arsil, and Qurrata Ayuni. "Models of Simultaneous Elections around the World: The Influence of Government Systems on Election Implementation Methods." *International Conference for Democracy and National Resilience (ICDNR 2023)*. Atlantis Press, 2023.
27. G.P. Srivastva, Curbing Booth Capturing and Election Rigging in India, *The Indian Journal of Public Administration*, Vol. XXXVII July-September, 1991 No.3, PP 475-484
28. George, A. Shaji. "One Nation, One Election: An Analysis of the Pros and Cons of Implementing Simultaneous Elections in India." *Partners Universal International Research Journal* 2.3 (2023): 40-60.
29. Gill, Manohar Singh. "India: running the world's biggest elections." *Journal of Democracy* 9.1 (1998): 164-168.
30. Gilmartin, David, and Robert Moog. "Introduction to "Election law in India"." *Election Law Journal* 11.2 (2012): 136-148.
31. Hakim, Fathurohman, and Fifiana Wisnaeni. "State Law Dynamics in the Context of Indonesia's 2024 Simultaneous Regional Elections."

International Journal of Multicultural and Multireligious Understanding 11.7 (2024): 351-358.

32. Hummel, Patrick, and Brian Knight. "Sequential or Simultaneous Elections? A Welfare Analysis." *International Economic Review*, vol. 56, no. 3, 2015, pp. 851–87. *JSTOR*, http://www.jstor.org/stable/24517904. Accessed 1 Oct. 2024.
33. Improving Procedures and Administrative Measures for Elections, *The Indian Journal of Public Administration*, Vol. XXXVII July-September, 1991 No.3, PP 529-533
34. Iqbal Narain, Future of Democracy in India: Some Reflections in the Context of the Tenth Lok Sabha Poll Verdict, *The Indian Journal of Public Administration*, Vol. XXXVII July-September, 1991 No.3, PP 485-495
35. Irfanoglu, B., Shakun D. Mago, and Roman M. Sheremeta. "Sequential versus simultaneous election contests: An experimental study." *Working Paper*. 2011.
36. Jaytilak Guha Roy, Electoral Violence and Role of Law and Order Administration, *The Indian Journal of Public Administration*, Vol. XXXVII July-September, 1991 No.3, PP 383-391
37. Joseph, Sarah, and Gurpreet Mahajan. "Elections and democratic process in India." *Economic and Political Weekly* (1991): 1953-1955.
38. K. Seshadri, Democracy Misspelt?, *The Indian Journal of Public Administration*, Vol. XXXVII July-September, 1991 No.3, PP 282-287
39. Kamala Prasad, Free, Fair, Peaceful Election and the Administration, *The Indian Journal of Public Administration*, Vol. XXXVII July-September, 1991 No.3, PP 373-382
40. Kaushik, Arun Kumar, and Yugank Goyal. "The desirability of one nation one election in India: Simultaneous elections." *The Journal of Social, Political, and Economic Studies* 44.1/2 (2019): 110-120.
41. Khare, Shubhank. "One Nation One Election in India." *Issue 3 Int'l JL Mgmt. & Human.* 5 (2022): 1309.
42. Krishan Kumar, Resume on Constitutional and Legal Provisions on Administering Elections, *The Indian Journal of Public Administration*, Vol. XXXVII July-September, 1991 No.3, PP 504-512
43. Krishna Mohan Mathur, Administering Election in India—Some Random Reflections, *The Indian Journal of Public Administration*, Vol. XXXVII July-September, 1991 No.3, PP 416-430
44. Kumar, Sanjay. "Elections in India." *The Oxford Handbook of Indian Politics* (2024): 143.
45. Kumar, Sanjay. *Elections in India: An Overview*. Routledge India, 2021.
46. Kusum Lata Bhandari, Election and Electoral Reforms in India, *The Indian Journal of Public Administration*, Vol. XXXVII July-September, 1991 No.3, PP 331-334

47. M. Subramanian, Electoral Reform and the Voter, *The Indian Journal of Public Administration*, Vol. XXXVII July-September, 1991 No.3, PP 307-309
48. Major Recommendations to Improve Electoral System, *The Indian Journal of Public Administration*, Vol. XXXVII July-September, 1991 No.3, PP 522-528
49. Mathur, Krishna Mohan. "Administering Elections in India--Some Random Reflections." *Indian Journal of Public Administration* 37.3 (1991): 416-430.
50. N.R. Inamdar, Theoretical Approaches in Elections: Implications for Outcomes of Elections Administration in India, *The Indian Journal of Public Administration*, Vol. XXXVII July-September, 1991 No.3, PP 267-281
51. N.S. Gehlot, Election and the Role of Money Power in India, *The Indian Journal of Public Administration*, Vol. XXXVII July-September, 1991 No.3 PP 437-447
52. Nutan Sinha, Women Participation and Involvement in Election, *The Indian Journal of Public Administration*, Vol. XXXVII July-September, 1991 No.3, PP 496-503
53. One Nation, One Election: What every UPSC aspirant must know about the govt's plan for simultaneous polls in the country, Times of India, Sept 18, 2024, https://timesofindia.indiatimes.com/education/news/one-nation-one-election-what-every-upsc-aspirant-must-know-about-the-govts-plan-for-simultaneous-polls-in-the-country/articleshowprint/113463529.%E2%80%A6 accessed on Sept 20, 2024
54. P.V. Indiresan, Electing Representative, Responsible and Responsive Legislators, *The Indian Journal of Public Administration*, Vol. XXXVII July-September, 1991 No.3, PP 294-301
55. R.B. Jain, Political Broadcasting in India, *The Indian Journal of Public Administration*, Vol. XXXVII July-September, 1991 No.3 , PP 392-415
56. Ramashray Roy, What Ails Our Electoral System, *The Indian Journal of Public Administration*, Vol. XXXVII July-September, 1991 No.3, PP 288-293
57. Reddi, Agarala Easwara, and D. Sundar Ram. "Administering Clean and Fair Elections in India." *Indian Journal of Public Administration* 37.3 (1991): 310-323.
58. Rozi, Agus Fahrur, Ahmad Redi, and Azis Budianto. "Legal Review Of Simultaneous Elections From The Perspective Of The 1945 Basic Act." *ICLSSEE 2023: Proceedings of the 3rd International Conference on Law, Social Science, Economics, and Education, ICLSSEE 2023, 6 May 2023, Salatiga, Central Java, Indonesia.* European Alliance for Innovation, 2023.

59. 'Simultaneous elections were the norm...'Ram Nath Kovind defends "One Nation One Election', Oct 6, 2024, https://timesofindia.indiatimes.com/india/simultaneous-elections-were-the-norm-ram-nath-kovind-defends-one-nation-one-election/articleshow/113981126.cms
60. S.C. Vajpeyi, Two Aspects of Election Administration—Mitigating Booth Capture and Management of Counting, *The Indian Journal of Public Administration*, Vol. XXXVII July-September, 1991 No.3, PP 456-474
61. S.K. Chaturvedi, Electoral Reforms: An Agenda, *The Indian Journal of Public Administration*, Vol. XXXVII July-September, 1991 No.3, PP 324-330
62. S.N. Mishra, Dynamics and Dimensions of Panchayati Raj Elections, *The Indian Journal of Public Administration*, Vol. XXXVII July-September, 1991 No.3, PP 335-348
63. S.S. Sharma, Administrators and Schedule Castes' Participation in Election, *The Indian Journal of Public Administration*, Vol. XXXVII July-September, 1991 No.3 PP 431-437
64. S.S. Singh and Suresh Mishra, Powers of Election Commission: A Legal Perspective, *The Indian Journal of Public Administration*, Vol. XXXVII July-September, 1991 No.3, PP 361-372
65. Shriram Maheshwari, The Conscience Keeper of Indian Democracy: The Election Commission, *The Indian Journal of Public Administration*, Vol. XXXVII July-September, 1991 No.3, PP 349-360
66. Shrotriya, Eesha, and Shantanu Pachauri. "Simultaneous elections and flexible legislative terms: a constitutionally preferable approach." *Indian Law Review* 5.1 (2021): 106-138.
67. Siddiqui, Najeed Naved. "Elections in India-A Brief Analysis." *Issue 2 Int'l JL Mgmt. & Human.* 4 (2021): 2931.
68. Smiriti Kak Ramachandran, 'One Nation, One Election' plan on agenda for current term of NDA, *Hindustan Times*, September 16, 2024, p. 8
69. Sonawane, Manik. (2024)."Exploring the Feasibility of One Nation One Election Reform in India." *Mahratta*, Kesari Mahratta Trust, Volume-I, Issue-I, July-2024, http://mahratta.org/CurrIssue/July_2024/4.%20Exploring%20the%20Feasibility%20of%20One%20Nation%20One%20Election%20Reform%20in%20India-Dr.%20Manik%20Sonawane.pdf
70. Suryanto, Adi, et al. "Asymmetric Election: Political Decentralization As A Lesson Learnt From Indonesia 2019 Simultaneous Election Problems." *Jurnal Studi Pemerintahan* (2021): 220-241.
71. Swaminathan, Siddharth, and Suhas Palshikar. *Politics and society between elections: Public opinion in India's States.* Routledge India, 2020.
72. Syafei, Muhammad, and Muhammad Rafi Darajati. "Design of general election in indonesia." *Law Reform* 16.1 (2020): 97-111.

73. Tawa Lama-Rewal, Stephanie. "Studying elections in India: Scientific and political debates." *South Asia Multidisciplinary Academic Journal* 3 (2009).
74. Utama, Joel Dharma, Indra Perwira, and Ali Abdurrahman. "Judicial Review Analysis of the General Election Law Number 42 of 2008 and Implications for the 2019 Simultaneous Elections." *Melayunesia Law* 5.2: 196-206.
75. V.B. Singh, Multiplicity of Candidates in Elections: A Case for Upward Revision in Security Deposits, *The Indian Journal of Public Administration*, Vol. XXXVII July-September, 1991 No.3, PP 448-475
76. Verma, Arvind. "Policing elections in India." *India Review* 4.3-4 (2005): 354-376.
77. Waza, Aarif Mohd. "Assessing the Feasibility and Implications of Implementing One Nation One Election in India." *International Journal of Advanced Technology and Social Sciences (IJATSS)* 1.3 (2023): 185-196.
78. Willnat, Lars, and Annette Aw. "Elections in India: One billion people and democracy." *The Handbook of Election News Coverage around the World.* Routledge, 2009. 124-141.
79. Yadav, Shyamlal. How it was curtains on 'One Nation, One Election' after coalition era onset in 1967, *The Indian Express*, October 6, 2024, https://indianexpress.com/article/political-pulse/how-it-was-curtains-on-one-nation-one-election-after-coalition-era-onset-in-1967-9592775/
80. Yadav, Vaibhav. "Democracy and Simultaneous Elections." *Issue 2 Int'l JL Mgmt. & Human.* 5 (2022): 1330.

About the Author

Dr Sapna Chadah

She is presently working as Associate Professor in Constitutional & Administration Law at Indian Institute of Public Administration, New Delhi. She holds Masters in Law (LL.M) from University of Delhi and Ph.D in Law from Jamia Millia Islamia, Delhi. She has an experience of more than 15 years in the area of teaching, training, research and consultancy. Her major areas of interest include Constitutional Law, Administrative Law, Consumer Protection law and Policy, Environmental Management, Laws in Urban Management, Regulation of service sectors and Privatization.

She has authored/ edited more than 20 books/ monographs and contributed more than 50 research papers in journals of repute. She was associated with a number of research studies in the area of consumer protection and consumer welfare, RTI and Evaluation of various government schemes. She has organized more than 200 training programmes, workshops, seminars and conferences for various stakeholders.